MAKING THE MOST OF YOUR LIBRARY CAREER

MAKING THE MOST OF YOUR LIBRARY CAREER

Edited by
Lois Stickell
Bridgette Sanders

An imprint of The American Library Association

Chicago   2014

LOIS STICKELL is history and government documents librarian at J. Murrey Atkins Library, University of North Carolina at Charlotte in Charlotte, North Carolina. She received her MLS from Indiana University in Bloomington, Indiana. She has written about a slave revolt in South Carolina, and she and Bridgette Sanders received a grant to research student activism in the 1960s. She contributed a chapter about grants to the ALA book *The Frugal Librarian: Thriving in Tough Economic Times* by Carol Smallwood.

BRIDGETTE SANDERS is social sciences librarian at J. Murrey Atkins Library, University of North Carolina at Charlotte in Charlotte, North Carolina. She received her MLS from Atlanta University in Atlanta, Georgia. Her areas of interest are Africana Studies and Diversity. She and Lois Stickell have presented at several conferences, including the Southern Historical Association's annual conference and the Association for the Study of African American Life and History (ASALH).

Printed in the United States of America

18 17 15 14   5 4 3 2 1

Extensive effort has gone into ensuring the reliability of the information in this book; however, the publisher makes no warranty, express or implied, with respect to the material contained herein.

ISBNs: 978-0-8389-1186-0 (paper); 978-0-8389-9598-3 (PDF); 978-0-8389-9599-0 (ePub); 978-0-8389-9600-3 (Kindle).

Library of Congress Cataloging-in-Publication Data

Making the Most of Your Library Career / edited by Lois Stickell and Bridgette Sanders.

   p.   cm

   Includes bibliographical references and index.

   ISBN 978-0-8389-1186-0 (alk. paper)

   1. Library science—Vocational guidance—United States. 2. Librarians—Employment—United States. 3. Librarians—United States—Interviews.

4. Career development. I. Stickell, Lois, 1951- editor of compilation.

II. Sanders, Bridgette, 1962- editor of compilation.

Z682.35.V62M33 2014

020.23—dc23   2013028023

Cover design by Kimberly Thornton. Image © Shutterstock, Inc.

Text design and composition by Ashley Paggi in the Chaparral Pro & Century Gothic typefaces.

CONTENTS

PREFACE

This is the book we wish had existed when we started our library careers. It could have saved us some missteps and might even have changed the direction of our careers. To compile this book, we recruited ten from-the-trenches librarians to offer practical insights into how to better launch and manage your library career:

- **Chapter 1** looks at first impressions through the interview process and during the first days on the job. While you are busy finding your footing, others are watching you and forming impressions that may be hard to change later. How you manage your early days on the job may influence your career for a long time.

- **Chapter 2** provides views from two library directors about the qualities they look for in candidates.

- **Chapter 3** offers advice for handling the unanticipated in your new work environment. This chapter includes lessons learned from a new manager and a frank look at some of the things she would do differently.

- **Chapter 4** looks at ways to assess your new workplace to determine if there is a need for change and offers suggestions on ways to make changes diplomatically. It also addresses the minefield of toppling long-standing procedures and advises how to determine when or if to initiate changes.

- **Chapter 5** examines the value of professional associations for your career. Will they further your career or are they too time consuming? Do they fit your interests and meet the approval of your supervisors?

- **Chapter 6** focuses on the cyclical nature of a librarian's year and advises how to manage your work more effectively. All libraries have peaks and lulls in workload that can bounce you from feeling overwhelmed to feeling bored. How you allot your time throughout the year can help you retain balance.

- **Chapter 7** tells how to evaluate and prioritize your workload and gives advice on when to step back and say no. Many of us try to do too much, but this may not be best for us or our fellow employees. Taking a step back and determining where your energies are best used can benefit you and your library.

- **Chapter 8** addresses using library school skills to find jobs outside of the library field. The writer developed a Plan B for finding a job when she couldn't get a job in a library. By assessing the skills she learned in library school, she was able to market herself in an entirely different field.

- **Chapter 9** looks at unconventional library jobs and how to find your niche inside or outside of a library building. Some people love librarianship but don't love the bureaucracy and want more independence.

- **Chapter 10** takes a hard look at moving on when a job doesn't work out. Even a good job may not be the right job for you. How you handle yourself when the job isn't working out may affect your future employment.

While some things can be learned only by experience, there are many things that others can teach you. We believe that practical advice from seasoned librarians is invaluable, especially in this changing environment, and we thank each author for contributing to this book. It really is the sum of its parts, and we are grateful for such strong, wise authors who were willing to share their knowledge and expertise.

The ways to success are as varied as people. This book was written to help new and future librarians formulate an organized approach to finding their career path.

Lois Stickell and Bridgette Sanders

FIRST IMPRESSIONS

Melinda Livas

Once the interview is over and you have the job, you will be dealing with many first impressions. Some of them are your own impressions of your new work environment; others are your colleagues' impressions of you. What you do and say in the early days of your employment can impact the smoothness of your work life for the next several years. This chapter explores first impressions through the interview process and during those first days on the job.

GETTING MY FIRST LIBRARIAN JOB

While attending graduate school, I was fortunate to work part time as a library assistant in an academic library. This gave me my first impressions of how a library operates, and I was able to observe librarians in their element. This experience also gave me a glimpse of what to expect from my first job as an academic librarian. Although every academic library has its own unique culture, this experience provided a frame of reference.

Unfortunately, I was finishing library school just as the economy was in a tailspin and educational budgets were being obliterated. Knowing that the job market for librarians had become exceptionally competitive made for a stressful final semester. However, I decided to use that semester to do everything possible to increase my chances of getting a job after I graduated. So, in essence, I began working on my first impression before I ever met any potential employers. One of the ways I did that was to convince two librarians in the academic library where I worked to let me co-teach some of their library instruction classes. This was a great learning experience because I was working alongside experienced library instructors. The experience also gave me the confidence to teach library instruction to large groups of students and prepared me for a presentation during an interview. Finally, it helped me stay abreast of the latest Web 2.0 technology tools and gave me ways to embed the tools in my class assignments and presentations.

Another way that I prepared myself for future interviews was by attending library candidates' presentations. I was able to extract ideas from all of the presentations I attended. I knew that I would be applying for jobs in academic libraries, and I knew that I would probably have to give a presentation as part of my job interview. Even if you don't work in a library, it still might be possible to attend a job interview presentation while you are in library school. Talk to a librarian at the type of library you are interested in working in and ask for a contact in human resources or the head of a department. It is so much easier to know what to expect once you have seen an interview presentation or two.

In addition to listening to the presentation, I observed each candidate's demeanor. One thing I learned was to smile and appear pleasant. While this may seem simple enough that it does not need to be stated, many candidates were so tense and nervous that they appeared upset or unpleasant. My impression was that this made everyone slightly uncomfortable. The candidates with a smile put people at ease.

MAKING GOOD IMPRESSIONS IN THE INTERVIEW

A month before graduating, I applied for a position at a small academic library. I was excited when I was asked to do a phone interview. I practiced answering library-related interview questions, and I studied the library's website to familiarize myself with their offerings and services. During the interview I focused on remaining calm and speaking clearly and at a moderate pace. I tried to answer each question thoroughly, despite being very nervous. There were five academic professionals interviewing me. Throughout the interview I tried to "read" the interviewers to gauge how well I was doing. I thought that I had made a good impression. I must have, because I received a call later on during the week to schedule a face-to-face interview.

On the interview day I arrived early because I know being late can leave a bad impression on a lot of people. I had my PowerPoint presentation uploaded to my flash drive and was ready to go. I knew that was important, too, because nothing tries peoples' patience like watching someone fumble to get a presentation going in front of a room full of people. I thought I did a fine job, but I was not offered the position.

While disappointing, it was also a moment for me to realize that my impression of myself was as important as that of potential employers. I needed to focus on the positive, and one positive from a failed interview was that it better prepared me for future interviews by giving me additional questions to practice on. My second interview was more successful, and I was offered the position.

The job was at a small, private academic institution. Having worked exclusively in a large academic library, I was unsure how I would adjust to such a small staff. My first day on the job was a whirlwind. The human resources orientation was long but useful. I made a point to smile at everyone. It is always important to appear friendly, but it may be even more important in a small institution because the people you meet outside the library are likely to know your new colleagues. You don't want anyone saying, "Your new hire seems aloof."

Tips for a Good Interview

- Practice answering library-related interview questions.
- Study the library's website to become familiar with offerings and services.
- Arrive early.
- Have your presentation ready to go.
- Remain calm and speak clearly during the interview.
- Answer questions thoroughly.

MAKING GOOD IMPRESSIONS WITH COWORKERS

Within the first few days I also made a point of sitting down with each of my new coworkers, even those with whom I did not work directly, to get an understanding of how their skills contributed to the library's operation. I knew that my new colleagues were watching to see how I fit in and to determine if I was going to create any problems. There is always a period of adjustment when someone new is added to a staff. That adjustment can be even more critical with a smaller staff. I made a point to hang back the first few days to observe how the others interacted. My goal was to be a team player, but first I had to figure out where I fit into the team. Every single day was not paradise, but when unpleasant situations arose—and they did—we respected one another enough to resolve the situation politely. This conflict resolution process was already part of the culture of the organization, so it was easy for me to go with that flow. However, if you find yourself in a tense situation, be careful not to take sides or further contribute to those tensions. Especially make sure that you are not drawn into gossip. Instead, try to maintain a neutral status and focus on the work to be done.

My day-to-day tasks involved working with six other librarians. I knew that each had an area of expertise, and I was careful not to overstep any boundaries because I knew that would create a bad impression. For instance, when I had technology questions, I always asked the IT (information technology) expert for advice instead of developing my own solutions. We would sit down and brainstorm the pros and cons of introducing a particular new technological service to our patrons and try to ascertain the implications. If the pros outweighed the cons, we took those ideas to the director as a team. This way we were sharing in both the possible praise and the possible rejection. When striving to make a positive impression, it's important to show that you are willing to put yourself on the line. If the cons outweighed the pros, then we would put those ideas aside until we could conjure up more pros. Making sure I always followed this process strengthened my relationships with coworkers.

> ### Tips for Making Good Impressions With Coworkers
>
> - Sit down with coworkers to understand how their skills contribute to library operations.
> - Observe how others interact.
> - Do not take sides in tense situations.
> - Focus on work to be done. Do not engage in gossip.
> - Do not overstep boundaries. Work together and share ideas.
> - Show initiative and innovation without stealing the limelight from others.
> - Participate in new projects.

Sometimes when you are trying to make a good first impression, you need to show initiative and innovation without seeming to constantly seek out or steal the limelight from others. For instance, as the distance services librarian, I thought it would be useful for me to know what type of technological platforms our distance learning students were using to access our online resources. With this in mind, I created a technology survey designed to ascertain the following: the type of Internet connectivity they used from home, whether it was dial-up, broadband, or DSL (digital subscriber line), and whether they used a regular cell phone or a smartphone. My results indicated that in order to successfully reach our distance learners, the library staff had to provide resources through a multitude of technological platforms, such as laptops, tablet computers, and smartphones. This initiative showed my supervisor that I was serious about my job, and I believe it confirmed her impression of me as a serious employee. It also allowed me to engage in some meaningful research that made me feel more positive about my job.

Another way to create and maintain a good relationship with new colleagues is to participate in new projects. When the Friends of the Library group contributed $40,000 to finance a much-needed quiet room, the collection management librarian orchestrated a massive weeding project. I participated with my colleagues in creating enough space to build a cozy quiet space in the library. I found that working together on this project helped create stronger ties.

It would be dishonest to pretend that being friendly and a good worker will win over every colleague. We have all worked with others who are challenging and who will, frankly, not engage with us or like us no matter how hard we try. If you perceive that you may have difficulty working with a particular coworker, observe to see how others deal with this individual. It is seldom the case that someone is a problem only for you. Sometimes it is necessary to acknowledge that we don't have a positive working relationship with everyone and move on. The key is to attempt to create good impressions and good working relationships with as many people as possible. If it doesn't work, well, at least you tried.

YOUR FIRST IMPRESSIONS

Along with making sure that you are putting your best foot forward in your new job, you should also assess your new environment and form your own judgments and impressions. Is the job what you expected? Do you believe that you will work well with your new coworkers? Are there unexpected parts to the job that you like or don't like? Are there job expectations that require skills you don't have?

No job can be perfectly represented during a job interview, and it is up to you in those first days and weeks of employment to learn your new environment in greater detail. This isn't simply an academic exercise. This is the time to ascertain that you really can do the job. If you realize you don't have a necessary set of skills, talk with your supervisor about training. Yes, it may feel a little awkward if he or she believed that you already possessed those skills, but it is far better to be honest than to try to bluff your way through.

Most positions are probationary for the first few months. Although no one wants to consider that he or she may have made a mistake and accepted a position that isn't right, it does happen. The early days are the time to gain a true impression of your work environment and colleagues and to make certain that this is the place for you. If your new situation is not going to work, you need to determine this sooner rather than later. More to the point, you want to be the one to make the choice to leave rather than have someone tell you that you aren't working out and should leave.

In most cases, your new job is the job you applied for and is where you want to stay. However, some job responsibilities are bound to be more complex than you anticipated or are performed differently than in your previous institution. The more carefully you observe and make your own first impressions, the better able you will be to learn the new system quickly. This will make you feel more comfortable and will reassure your supervisor that the right choice was made in hiring you.

MAKING A GOOD IMPRESSION ACROSS CAMPUS

Initially, the hardest part of my job was reaching out to the faculty members, especially the adjunct faculty members because they did not have a physical space on campus. My main objective was to deliver a library instruction session or sessions to *all* communication classes, undergraduate and graduate. I realized that this was an ambitious goal but, as the information fluency librarian, it was my responsibility to market information fluency to the entire university community, both face-to-face and virtually.

I began by writing an e-mail for the faculty members in the School of Communication. I included a brochure that explained the services I could provide. I was careful to make sure the brochure looked professional and was a good introduction of myself to the faculty. I believe that I created a positive first impression with this brochure, and I was rewarded when several faculty members asked me to give library instruction sessions.

That led to step two. Although I had "met" the faculty and created an impression virtually, it was important to maintain that good first impression once I entered their classrooms. Before teaching a library instruction class, I made a point to sit down with the professor and find out what he or she expected from the session. This was my first face-to-face meeting with the professor. I always arrived on time and dressed professionally. These are small things, but they do matter. After meeting with the professor, I customized an instruction session relevant to the students' assignments. Although I may have impressed the professor, I knew that once I entered the classroom I needed to make a good impression on the students. The way to do that was to offer them something of value and to do it in a way that let them know I was approachable and available to assist them with their needs. Because I know it is important to keep students engaged, I always include some hands-on projects during the library instruction session. This gives students a concrete and visual learning experience and allows me to move around the room and talk with them, rather than remaining a remote instructor at the front of the class.

While it was important that I make a good impression on the faculty and students, I was also making my own judgments and forming my own impressions. Was this a professor with whom I believe I could work on a research project? Could I embed myself in this particular class, or were the dynamics wrong for that? Always bear in mind that impressions are a two-way street, and you must judge as well as be prepared to be judged.

SOCIAL NETWORKING IS MY FRIEND—RIGHT?

I created a fan page on Facebook for our library and posted library and campus events. Facebook and Twitter can be excellent tools for marketing the library. After creating a fan page on Facebook, I encouraged other professionals and students to follow us. This created another avenue to "meet" people and make a good impression by being where the students are.

While Facebook can be a marketing tool for a library, many people also have personal pages. It can be easy to become lax about personal Facebook pages and allow our personal and professional lives to become intertwined. When it comes to creating impressions about yourself, nothing is more damaging than posting unflattering remarks online pertaining to your workplace or coworkers. You may believe that you are safe in doing so because no one at work is your friend on Facebook. However, people know people who know people. If you say something derogatory, there is a very good chance it will be seen by the wrong people. You could hurt your working relationships with coworkers without ever realizing why they no longer seem as friendly or supportive. Recently, teachers and other workers have gained media attention for inappropriate comments about work or fellow workers. Librarians should be aware of the need for discretion. Before you post something, ask yourself if you would want to see that particular comment aimed at you. That doesn't mean you can't mention your library in a Facebook posting. You can. Say something positive about your library or some display currently available there, but avoid mentioning anyone by name.

THE NEXT STOP

One day, out of the blue, I received an e-mail from a friend about a job at another library. To be honest, another job was the furthest thing from my mind because I was doing well at my current job. I had developed an excellent working relationship with my coworkers, and my research projects were beginning to flourish. However, after reading the job description, I was intrigued.

The position encompassed using technology to teach library instruction via distance education. I believe that learning how to use new technological tools is the best part about being a librarian. A job that implemented new technologies to enhance a library user's experience appealed to me. So I applied and two weeks later participated in a phone interview. Once again, I had to focus on making a good first impression. I find phone interviews more challenging than face-to-face interviews because you can't see the other parties to determine how you are doing. I was exceptionally nervous. Although I did not believe I did very well, I was invited to an on-campus interview with the director and the search committee. It was a challenging interview with a lot of questions. Many of the questions required lengthy responses. I focused on making sure I gave the best answer possible to each question, even when I felt myself tiring. After all, this was my one and only chance to make the right impression to get the job. The strategy worked and I was offered the position.

I found leaving my first librarian job bittersweet. While I was thrilled to embark on the second phase of my career, it was hard to tell my current colleagues good-bye because we had created such a good team. I knew that I was going to have to learn another set of personalities and begin the process of building partnerships in a completely new environment. This was both exciting and daunting.

Once I knew that I would be leaving, I resolved to be present until I actually left. It may be tempting to slack off as a job is tapering down, but I advise resisting that temptation. I wanted to perform up to my usual standards until the end. After all, I was still creating impressions, even if they were no longer first impressions, and I didn't want people to remember me as the person who left a lot of unfinished projects.

CREATING GOOD FIRST IMPRESSIONS WITH A MORE DIVERSE GROUP

Unlike my previous group of coworkers, most of the librarians at my new institution were men. The librarians were also very culturally diverse. I knew this might mean adapting to different communication styles. I began my first days at work by paying particular attention to how the staff interacted with one another, taking my cues from them.

After getting to know my new coworkers, I set up a meeting with the distance learning director. She shared her vision for my involvement with the distance coordinators as well as ideas to enhance the services already in place from the previous distance librarian. While I knew that my working relationship with her was important, it was vital that I work collaboratively with the coordinators if I wanted to be successful as the distance services librarian. The coordinators would connect me to their adjunct faculty members, who in turn would connect me to our distance students. This was my first realization that first impressions can have a domino effect. If I made a good impression with the director, it was probable that she would pass the word along that I was easy to work with and open to new ideas. Similarly, every time I had contact with adjunct faculty members, there was every possibility they would pass along their impressions of me to their fellow adjuncts and to their students.

The distance learning director facilitated monthly coordinators' meetings. This was the perfect venue for me to meet the coordinators. I was excited about that because it meant I could create one killer presentation for the entire group. However, I soon learned that some of the coordinators did not attend these meetings. This meant I would have to contact and create a favorable impression with them in other ways. I sent them an introductory e-mail outlining the services I intended to provide to them and their students. Initially, I didn't receive any responses from the coordinators, which was disheartening and frustrating. I soldiered on and continued to reach out to the coordinators.

Approximately a month later, I received a library instruction request from one of the distance coordinators who manages one of our largest distance learning programs. We met and mapped out a plan for me to provide a library instruction session to all seven of her off-site distance locations. By working closely with her and letting her take the lead on future collaborations, I made a good impression as a team player.

Although this eventually worked out positively, it's unrealistic to believe that you will achieve success every time. In reality, not every situation turns out well. Not every professor is interested in having a librarian speak to his or her class and will ultimately reject any effort. During the times I was unsuccessful in creating partnerships, I reminded myself that I had made my best effort. That is all that can be expected in any work situation.

THE NEW KID ON THE BLOCK

I have been in my current position for almost a year, and I am no longer the new kid on the block. However, this does not mean that I can afford to become so relaxed that I no longer care about the opinions people have of me. I continue to care and I try not to do things that cause colleagues to negatively revise their opinions of me.

As a new librarian, make sure you understand your job and perform it well. Step out of your comfort zone and try different things. If you can, volunteer to work on departmental committees outside of the library as a way to learn the culture of your environment. Your work represents you better than any brochure you can write, and word of mouth is a powerful marketing tool. Making sure that you perform well is the essence of creating a good first impression and making it a lasting impression.

2

THE VIEW FROM THE TOP

Theodosia Shields and Annie Payton

One of the most intimidating things a new graduate, or even an experienced librarian, can do is to interview for a job. Part of the apprehension is because a candidate does not know what the library director is looking for and what types of things will impress a library director. This chapter tries to take some of the uncertainty out of the interview process by providing the views from two experienced library directors.

PREPARING FOR NEW HIRES

Every library director is looking for the ideal employee, but it can be challenging and time consuming to find this person. As two library directors who have experienced the ups and downs of managing employees from diverse cultures and backgrounds, we have developed some strategies and insights that help us know when a potential employee is a good fit. We have also had to develop interventions to use when an employee is no longer a good fit. Although our views may not be universally accepted, they offer a starting point for thinking about how library directors may view you as a candidate and an employee.

The decision about what type of person to hire for a certain position begins long before the interview. A library director devotes time to thinking about expectations for a new hire. Every director has expectations about the skills a new employee must bring to the organization to meet the library's needs. Once the decision has been made to recruit for a new position and a job description written, a human resources department will review the application. While human resources departments may be invisible to most candidates, they do exist and serve a valuable function in the job-posting process. They make certain the job description is clean and accurate. They can also make determinations that a candidate is not qualified, so be certain that you follow the job requirements when applying or your application could be pulled before anyone at the library ever sees it.

Another important factor is the question of seasoned versus inexperienced. The library landscape has changed and continues to evolve. Job titles and responsibilities are reviewed regularly and are often repurposed to fit the changing needs of the library. The delivery of library services and programs continues to shift toward the technology side. While seasoned librarians bring "over-the-years-experience" that cannot be gained in classrooms, seasoned librarians may not possess the technology skills the position demands. An inexperienced employee may bring the technology skills and enthusiasm but lack the experience to balance those. Most library directors are hoping to find a good combination of experience and technology skills. That doesn't mean library directors pass over new graduates who have no paid work experience. It means your résumé should include some volunteer experience or solid course work. Some jobs simply require a person who has done the job before, especially if there is no one available to do training. However, this would be clearly noted on the job posting, so there should not ever be an issue of someone who does not have the required experience being invited to an interview.

Once a job has been posted, the director defers to a search committee for much of the frontline work in filling that position. The library director generally meets with the search committee to give guidance and articulate expectations for the new hire. Most library directors will then allow the committee to screen for best-fit candidates. The search committee reads letters of interest and résumés and selects the top choices. This is when the library director reenters the process.

RÉSUMÉS MATTER

Good library directors pay close attention to the résumés of the final candidates. Unfortunately, most MLS (master of library science) résumés read very much the same. While it can be hard to distinguish yourself in a résumé, try to include some significant aspect about yourself or your work experience. We look for candidates who stand out with unique skills that could be beneficial to the library. For instance, a candidate for reference who also has public relations experience has assets that make us take a second look. The candidate does not need extensive experience, but something as simple as an internship or course work in a desired area could precipitate an interview.

On the subject of résumés, long ones are never advisable. These do not impress the committee and are not likely to get passed on to the library director. Rather, they send a signal that the applicant is not able to be concise and cannot highlight his or her most significant achievements succinctly. We have read résumés where a candidate lists achievements from fifteen and twenty years ago or lists far too many accomplishments. Including too much information may cause a reader to miss something important in your résumé that would give you an advantage over other candidates. Be judicial in what you choose to include. It is also helpful to group experience and skills under separate subject headings rather than placing them together. Remember, you want to present yourself as positively and simply as possible. When there are many applicants for a position, even the smallest misstep can lead to your being eliminated from consideration.

> ## Tips for an Ideal Résumé
>
> - Skip the "Objective" statement.
> - Give short, sharp details to make it less generic.
> - Use action verbs—descriptions such as "I was assigned" give the impression of lack of motivation.
> - Use bullet points and run a spell-check.
> - Focus on your most recent job(s).

In today's world, every library director is looking for an individual who can be flexible. The job that you are hired for today will probably change, sometimes drastically, over the next three years. Libraries are changing very rapidly, and every part of the library is changing with them. While we are not going to make new IT (information technology) persons work on the reference desk, we will expect that they are able to rethink their position as the needs of the library change. It is therefore important to show that you possess flexibility, so be sure to include past examples of this on your résumé.

Up until this point, the only knowledge a library director receives about a candidate is information presented on the résumé. Be neat, concise, and informative. Easy, huh?

INTERVIEWS

After the initial screening process has taken place, several candidates may be selected for phone interviews. The top candidates are then typically invited to in-person interviews. Once the candidates are actually present, the entire library observes to determine how a candidate might fit into the organization. This is the moment when a candidate is being introduced to thirty different people, smiling, shaking hands, and trying to sort out who is who. It's fine to tell someone later in the day—or five minutes later—"I'm sorry, I forgot your name." We realize that you are overwhelmed. It is appreciated, though, if you have spent some time beforehand familiarizing yourself with the library and staff. Then when you are introduced to Jane Doe, you can say, "Oh, you're in Information Commons."

As a rule, candidates are asked to give a presentation to the staff or the campus community. This is often one of the most nerve-racking parts of an interview for a candidate because everyone is watching and judging. The library director in particular listens for content knowledge, watches to see how comfortable the candidate is with others, determines whether the candidate listens to and answers questions, and gauges how interested the candidate appears in the organization.

Questions To Expect at an Interview

- Why do you want this job? (Hint: Include in your answer an aspect of the job you are interviewing for, not "I've always wanted to work in a library.")
- What will you bring to the job?
- What was the most challenging work situation you faced and how did you handle it?
- Where do you see yourself in five years?
- What are your strengths and weaknesses?

There are certain time-honored questions most candidates are asked at every interview. Although it can be tempting to regard these as boilerplate questions, most library directors take them seriously and listen closely to the responses. Library directors have heard these questions answered a number of times and look for certain key elements. As a candidate, try to avoid canned responses to these standard questions. Instead, make the answers your own while still addressing the question. Short, targeted examples are always helpful. A certain amount of library jargon is expected, but don't go overboard with it.

For instance, almost every interviewer asks a candidate if he or she is a team player. We want to hear the interviewees articulate philosophies about how they work with others. "Yes, I am a team player" is not a sufficient answer. How? Give examples. The responses help a library director determine if candidates have personal agendas they are seeking to advance. We generally pursue the "I am a team player" answer with additional questions to ascertain whose team you are on; that is, whose agenda will receive focus—yours or ours? Since each library entity is dependent on the others, it is important that everyone works together to fulfill library goals. In a well-run library, employees share interdependent goals. This helps ensure that the employees and library directors navigate on the same agenda. If we determine a candidate has a different focus and will not be able to fully engage in the library's goals, it is a clear signal that this is not the right person.

You are also likely to be asked, "Why do you want this job?" Your answer should be related to the job; for example, "I've always wanted to focus on technology, and this position offers me the chance to use my expertise." While we realize that candidates may also have personal reasons, do not say that you want the position because your family lives nearby.

You will be asked several times throughout the day if you have questions. Often you will be asked the same question more than once. This is not designed to trip you up to see if you answer the same each time. The questions are probably from two different people. It's fine to say, "As I told Sally earlier . . ." and then include something more: "I'd also add that . . ."

If you have questions, by all means ask them. This is not just about people making decisions about you. You are the primary decider here and should be determining if this is the right job for you. If you don't have questions, say politely, "Not at the moment." However, anyone who goes through the entire day without asking questions is sending a signal that he or she is not very interested in the position. If you believe you are interested, or even if you are not sure, ask some questions. Maintain a calm, friendly demeanor even if the interview does become tiring. Everyone there has been through the process and they empathize, but they also want to see how you perform under a certain amount of stress.

In the end, making a determination about a candidate comes down to a gut reaction for most library directors. We ask ourselves, "Do I believe that this person has the skills and traits I am looking for in a particular position? Do I believe this person will work well with others?" Working well with others really supersedes all other characteristics. The most brilliant subject specialist who is difficult and who will bring a lot of high drama to the library is simply not going to work. This doesn't mean we demand an extrovert. Introverts are fine as long as they can fulfill the requirements of the job. We are looking for the individual who will bring the least amount of drama into the workplace. We are here to accomplish a job, and we have our antennae up for those who will make accomplishing that job more challenging.

THE PERSONAL INTERVIEW WITH THE DIRECTOR

At some point, often at the end of the day when you may be feeling exhausted, you will meet with the library director. This is the moment you have been waiting for. You finally have the opportunity to speak privately with the person who will make the final decision to hire or not hire you. No pressure. Okay, so there is some pressure. Just be pleasant and let the library director take the lead.

The director has carefully selected questions to determine what you can bring to the organization and to the people that the organization is expected to serve. This is your opportunity to prove to the director that you are the right person for the position. One key point to remember is to give a straightforward answer to each question. As simple as that may seem, it does not always happen. Don't stray into answering the question you wish the library director had asked or veer off track onto a favorite topic. Be clear and concise. If you finish and sense the library director is waiting for more, then elaborate but without droning on. In addition to answering questions, listen carefully to what the director says. You want to leave the interview with as much knowledge as possible about the organization so that you can make the appropriate decision about whether this is the right job for you. If you have questions that have not been addressed, this is the time to ask them.

Good library directors want to guide and help employees find their voice, as opposed to instructing them in what to do. We call it providing a blueprint for creativity. We give them broad direction and they fill in the details. We are always listening in the interview to determine whether a candidate has the ability to self-direct while still working within the blueprint we provide. From the candidate's perspective, this can feel challenging. You must convince us that you are able to work independently while still staying within a framework.

At the same time that we are making personal judgments about a candidate, we are very aware of our responsibility to the candidate. It is important for the library director to share his or her vision. This is an opportunity for the candidate to consider whether the library director's vision is in sync with his or her own vision. When we talk about management style and expectations, it is to let the candidate know what to expect if he or she is offered a position. That candidate needs to consider whether we share the same vision before he or she accepts a position. Be sure you listen carefully instead of thinking about your own next question.

Interview Questions to Expect from a Library Director

- What is your work style? (E.g., prefer to work alone or on a team.)
- How do you handle conflict with coworkers? Can you give an example of how you have implemented this?
- What is the worse work-related mistake you have made and how did you resolve it?
- What is the first thing you would do if given a team to lead?
- Can you give examples of projects you have worked on with others inside and outside the library?
- Are you willing to ask for help if you feel uncertain? Can you tell me about the last time you did this?

Beyond the basics of seeking an employee with the right expertise and attitude, a good library director is always looking for someone who has leadership potential. Leadership is not limited to managers. We seek this skill in all potential employees. Leadership is more than being able to get out in front and direct others. It is also the ability to lead from any position and to have ideas and be innovative in the job, whether the job is as a cataloger or a library instruction coordinator. Leadership includes a quality of enthusiasm that, frankly, no library director can give an employee. It has to come from within, and it has to be there from the start. When we interview candidates, we look for this quality.

A good leader knows when to "stay in your lane." We have had dedicated workers who overstep boundaries. This leads to a domino effect of personnel problems. As library directors, we want someone with that spark who will take a leadership position in whatever job he or she is hired for but who will also be respectful of others' authority. If this sounds complicated, it is. Each library director is essentially trying to predict the future when sizing someone up and determining how or if that person will fit well. Good candidates can make the job of predicting future results easier by being honest about their skills. It's okay to say, "I've had some experience with Drupal, but I am not an expert." If you finish by saying, "But I'm certainly willing to learn," we will be impressed.

HIRING FOR THE MANAGEMENT TRACK

When hiring for a management position, a library director looks for a manager who supports the library's goals even if he or she does not agree with them. Managing involves the employee understanding where the responsibilities of the operations of the library or organization rest. Therefore, a good manager assists the leadership in carrying out the daily functions of the library's services and programs. The manager helps set the environment for the work flow of those daily functions. The manager is often the employee whom the public, students, and faculty see. For library directors, managers serve as buffers. Managers help library leadership solve problems or reach a consensus.

While a manager may possess knowledge of the profession, he or she must also have maturity. This attribute may not be readily apparent, and often the search committee and the library director have to ask selected questions designed to give insight on the maturity level of the individual. Information regarding leadership maturity can also be gathered from the candidate's references and work experiences.

Whether looking for a professional librarian or support staff, we value the ability to negotiate, navigate, and network. The employee must be able to negotiate with the library director for simple requests such as time off, supplies, travel, and so forth. Sometimes employees perceive that another employee is favored when actually the employee was simply a better negotiator. Library directors know that an employee who can astutely negotiate with them can also negotiate skillfully with vendors and sales representatives. In the library profession, this is a valued asset.

In addition, every employee should possess the ability to navigate through and around the system of policies and procedures. While we don't expect candidates to know specific university policies, we do observe for the critical thinking skills necessary to learn and follow policies and procedures.

We also value a manager who understands the art of networking. Networking often continues in informal settings after five or at library conferences. While social networking has impacted face-to-face contact, young librarians should understand that meeting someone in person is a powerful way to make an impression. Friendly conversation, a handshake, and a smile all contribute positively to the impression you make on people. Sometimes things get done in a job because you are able to pick up the phone and make a personal request. Networking can also be beneficial to your career. While not everyone you meet may impact your career, you are building a network of potential colleagues. The library world is also a small world, and someone you may not even remember meeting could very well say something positive about you that could lead to an interview or a hire.

YOUR ROLE AFTER YOU LAND THE JOB

Communication is an essential factor for new hires as well as long-term staff. Open, honest communication with the director and middle management is crucial to the success of the organization. This is one of the most important pieces of information we share with prospective hires. If a candidate does not ask about our communication style in the interview, we bring it up. A candidate can have excellent technology and content knowledge skills, but if he or she is not able to communicate within the hierarchy, there could problems. Effective communication is necessary to prevent frustration and to keep everyone working together smoothly.

Acceptable or preferred lines of communication should be discussed with the new hire and/or staff. We always ask candidates how they prefer to communicate, as this provides insight into their preferred mode of communicating and lets us determine whether this would work for the organization. These venues also present an effective path for new hires or staff to share their vision and ideas for the organization.

The new employee also should not wait for a formal meeting to have a conversation or bring a matter to the attention of the director if needed. Open communication is a mutual responsibility. The employee must be willing to share with the director. At the same time, most library directors are very busy, so be judicious about setting up an appointment.

This does not mean that a new employee should be abandoned to flail around trying to find someone to answer questions. Each new employee should have a mentor. If you are not assigned one, ask for one. It sometimes happens that a new employee is assigned a mentor who either doesn't have the time or isn't interested in fulfilling the role. If this is the case for you, set up an appointment with the library director and request a different mentor. Rather than giving a play-by-play account of what went wrong, simply say, "I don't think this is a good fit. I was wondering if someone else could be assigned as my mentor."

A new employee should also know that most library directors don't want tension in the workplace. We aren't naive enough to think that everyone likes everyone else, but we do want civility maintained. If you don't care for someone, limit your time with this individual when possible. When you must interact or serve on a committee together, be polite and keep your personal feelings confined. You are in a business relationship and must behave in a businesslike manner. Believe me, a library director notices the people who work well with others, along with those who don't. When you are new to the job, it is essential that you be viewed as someone who can get along. You can go home at night and complain to your spouse if you want to, but don't go home and post your complaints on your Facebook page.

FINAL THOUGHTS

Every candidate should know that it is a tedious process to create a job description, advertise, review applicants' qualifications, and then conduct interviews. No library director wants to repeat this process because he or she made a mistake in hiring. While we may overlook a misstep or an ill-informed answer in an interview, we can't afford to ignore warning signs that indicate a candidate is the wrong choice. From the interviewer's perspective, a candidate should realize that he or she is being judged on everything he or she says or does. Yes, that text message you sent during our lunch may come back to haunt you. Be aware that you really must put your best foot forward because the library director is unlikely to take a chance on someone who commits too many missteps during the interview.

3

THE ACCIDENTAL LIBRARIAN

Tamara Acevedo

Almost every interview comes complete with a job description. We make choices about accepting a position based on how confident we feel about being able to perform the job as advertised. Often, however, job responsibilities change, or we move up the ladder and find ourselves in unfamiliar territory. This chapter looks at strategies for dealing with the unexpected in the work environment, including hard-learned lessons from a new manager.

MY PATH TO LIBRARIANSHIP

If someone had told me that a traffic violation would steer me toward the path of librarianship, I would have laughed out loud. It turns out that this is exactly what happened during my sophomore year of college. I was sentenced to attend driving school and perform thirty hours of community service for a reckless driving citation, and this is when I officially started my course to becoming an "accidental librarian."

I was told I could perform my community service in the library at UNC Charlotte in the Government Documents department. I was thrilled. The library was convenient because I lived on campus and my sentence was not going interfere with my classes. I planned to show up, do whatever I was told to do, and be done with it. I had used the library in my studies, but I had no idea what librarians actually did beyond checking out books and making sure that everyone kept quiet. I learned so much during those thirty hours, including where microfiche were kept and that there was actually a method to how they were filed. To my surprise, I found the work enjoyable. I was excited when I was able to answer another student's questions. My growing enthusiasm for the work must have made an impression on my supervisors, because after my involuntary tenure had ended, I was offered a position as a paraprofessional.

I accepted because I needed a job and because I now saw libraries in a much more favorable light. However, I thought that working in an academic library prepared me for work in any library. So, filled with confidence, I applied for a position as a library assistant at a large law firm. I got the job. That's when I received a rude awakening about the differences between academic, special, public, and government libraries.

> ## Accidental Librarians
>
> . . . are librarians without a formal education in library and information science, librarians with no professional library experience prior to becoming librarians, those who didn't set out to be librarians through the traditional channels.
>
> (Pamela H. MacKellar, "Introduction," in *The Accidental Librarian*, Medford, NJ: Information Today, 2008)

At that time, the firm did not have an electronic catalog. My new supervisor, the library manager, had been in her position about twenty years and had a wealth of knowledge stored in her head. She never seemed to have a problem finding anything. The firm had a nice-size library on one floor and smaller, satellite libraries on other floors. Books were grouped together by practice area but were not labeled or in any specific order. I was at a loss, and it took me a long time to learn where everything was kept. One thing that helped me learn was that I checked in periodicals and shelved books.

Another big difference I encountered in my new job was that there was a small staff. This was in direct contrast to the academic library, where there was a large staff and people assigned to do very specific tasks. In the law library, there were only three of us—and we were expected to do it all. Daily tasks included routing, reference, and circulation. After we purchased an automated system, we also cataloged and bar-coded materials.

I had never had any course work to prepare me for these duties, and I had no idea how to do the majority of them. It was all on-the-job training. I was overwhelmed, but I managed to survive. One of the key things I realized that helped me survive was that there are universal elements of library employment present in every type of library, whether it is a public, private, school, or government library. These elements include customer service, good communication, and training.

THE THREE BASICS OF ANY JOB

It did not take me long in my new position to realize that I was in a very different situation from the academic library I had left. At first I was nervous, but once I realized there are three key components to this or any job, I was able to approach the work differently. The most important component is good customer service. A library that has a fabulous collection but provides poor customer service is not going to be perceived well by its constituents.

Most professions include working with other people, or "customers," in some capacity. If your new patron base is unfamiliar to you, try drawing from previous experiences or encounters. I went from helping students to assisting attorneys and paralegals. Although it was tough to see at the time, at the bare bones, the principles of being courteous, respectful, attentive, and thorough were the same. In any library, excellent customer service is important, whether dealing with the public or patrons in a corporate setting.

Learning how to communicate with attorneys at the law library was definitely a skill that took time to develop. Although I didn't realize it, I was actually learning how to conduct a reference interview. Some attorneys at my firm came right out and asked for exactly what they needed. However, most approached me with very general questions. Finding out what they really wanted was like pulling teeth! I learned that every reference interview is different because each patron is different. I also learned the importance of finding out the context of the question and determining where the person has already looked for answers. In the beginning, I hesitated to question attorneys further when they seemed so sure of what they were looking for and where that information should be. After a while, I gained more confidence and learned to restate a complex question to ensure that I was clear about what they were seeking.

At the mention of training, the first thing that probably comes to mind is the librarian attending training to learn needed skills. The other side of that coin, training others, is also important. The more I offered and conducted training for our patron base, the more I learned for myself. Training others tests our knowledge and helps us learn about our patrons and their everyday research needs. It also shows us where we are weak and even where we need to do a better job at getting the word out about library resources. Another benefit of training is that it gives us an opportunity to interact with patrons one-on-one instead of simply exchanging e-mails. Sometimes spending time with an individual can give a better sense of his or her needs and how he or she expresses those needs.

GETTING UP TO SPEED QUICKLY

It's intimidating to find yourself in a new work situation where you have to figure out how to proceed. I found that the best way to address the problem is to use the people around you to learn. Engaging socially, perhaps by going to lunch, is probably the fastest way to learn the culture of your new employer and supervisor. Another way to learn is to pay attention to your new boss and follow his or her lead. In addition to learning about the organization, knowing what your supervisor wants and delivering it is the surest way to make him or her look good.

It's also helpful to maintain contact with former coworkers. The same reference librarian at the university who encouraged me to become a librarian was, and still is, a lifeline. In the beginning, I called her when I was clueless about how to find information. I still do. Also, keep the librarians at the public library in mind. When I was getting started, they went out of their way to help me and are still helpful today.

Another resource that is often overlooked is the human resources department. I discovered that they can provide reading materials and access to training opportunities. If you are new to a job, let the human resources personnel know your needs so that they can keep you informed of opportunities as they arise. They are also helpful in identifying other resources that could help you get up to speed quickly.

FIRST-TIME MANAGER

Although I enjoyed working at the law firm, I realized that I would not have the opportunity to advance. After a few years, I was ready for more responsibility and the chance for a bigger paycheck, so I decided to look for another job. I quickly learned that any move I made would most likely be a lateral one because I did not have a library science degree. This was disappointing because I saw myself as a working librarian. I liked the field, and I wanted to continue in it. I also wanted to advance. So, after five years as a paraprofessional, I enrolled in a program to get a master's degree in library science.

The classes went well and I learned a lot. I was in my last semester of library school when I was promoted to a managerial position. I was flattered and a little scared. It was the first time I had reported to someone who was not librarian.

I soon realized that being a manager was a whole new ball game, and I was not prepared for the role. In library school I had focused on becoming a reference librarian. I had not taken any classes in management, and I found myself lacking in some of the skills needed to be a manager.

One of my biggest challenges was managing people, especially those with whom I had worked alongside for several years. It was definitely awkward, and I admit I made mistakes. One of my mistakes was that I treaded very lightly at first because I did not want my new library technical assistant to feel like I was her boss. In my mind, we could continue the friendly relationship that we had enjoyed for more than eight years. It did not take long to realize that was not going to work. In order to get the work done, I had to make a change. Unfortunately, I compounded my first mistake with a second one: I failed to make a clear, strong statement about the changes I was initiating and what my new expectations were. Eventually I realized that I was in charge and I had to conduct myself as a manager and supervisor. I accepted that I would not always be popular and I could not always please everyone. Ultimately, I was fine with this because I wanted to advance up the ladder. However, it's a terrible thing to end up in a position and realize you don't want to be there. I advise not seeking a managerial position if you know yourself to be the type of person who is uncomfortable with criticism—both giving and receiving.

Because the reference librarian position I had vacated remained unfilled for an entire year, I was performing two jobs—department manager and reference librarian. In addition to answering reference questions, I had to find time to learn what the numbers on the spreadsheets meant. To be honest, learning accounting skills was my most difficult challenge that first year. I learned that multitasking may be a wonderful skill, but it can also become counterproductive if you never give a task your

---

Tips for Becoming a Successful Manager

- Learn to delegate. Do not try to do everything yourself.
- Select the right person for the job.
- Be clear when initiating change. Delineate expectations.
- Learn how to budget.
- Realize you cannot please everyone.
- Be accessible. Keep surprises to a minimum.
- Develop a relationship with other managers.
- Be visible to your patrons.

undivided attention. That first year as manager I worked all the time, but I was pulled in too many directions. Thankfully, I did not reach the point of burnout.

After a year, the firm hired a reference librarian, so I was no longer doing two jobs. This should have been a great relief, but it actually took a while to become comfortable with delegating work. I hadn't realized how bad my control issues were. I finally saw that it was a disservice not to delegate duties. I was hindering the growth of people who were perfectly capable of doing the job. As part of learning to delegate, a manager needs the ability to select the right person for the task. I had no experience with cultivating and choosing staff, and I suffered from the "must do everything" rule. I had to learn that a good manager is able to delegate work and then simply make sure the work gets done. Much of what I learned those early months was by trial and error. I still couldn't put my finger on exactly how to know the right person for the right job, but I will say it does become easier, and I believe my managers develop a "sense" for this.

Once I became comfortable with delegating, I had the time to concentrate on developing other managerial skills. Budgeting is a major duty for a manager or director. Library directors and managers must have accounting and expense management skills. Aside from a few accounting classes in college and handling my personal expenses, I had little experience in either. To get up to speed, I reviewed previous years' budgets and expenditures. I also picked up valuable tips from other librarians. One tip that was particularly helpful is to budget all year long. Now, at the end of every month, I review expenses and fill in my budget worksheet for the corresponding month for next year. Another excellent resource is the American Library Association's ALA Online Learning website (www.ala.org/onlinelearning/home). It offers a wide range of options for e-courses, including a section dedicated to courses on budgeting. Considering recent economic times with a lot of libraries forced to trim spending to the bare minimum, this is an important and timely topic.

NAVIGATING THE NEW DUTIES

I learned a lot from my new boss in my first few months. One of the first things he told me is that it is important in management to be accessible. He also told me to keep the surprises to a minimum. This let me know that, although he was not a micromanager and trusted my judgment, he wanted me to keep him in the loop.

I also found it beneficial to develop relationships with other managers in my firm. We shared the same boss even though we managed different departments. This allowed me to gain insight into my new supervisor's style, requirements, and expectations.

I also found myself performing other job duties that were new to me. One of them was negotiating contracts with vendors. Having never been a haggler, this was truly an eye-opening experience. My supervisor and I worked together negotiating large contracts with such vendors as Lexis and Westlaw. My supervisor taught me that the terms must be in the very best interest of your employer. If they are not, do not accept them. I also learned that everything is negotiable.

No matter how good a job you are doing and how well your library is run, if you are invisible to your patrons and aren't aware of this, you are failing. I came to understand the value of making the library visible when someone in another department purchased a very pricey product without consulting the librarians. I found out about the purchase when attorneys began calling for the log-in information. I was offended that no one even thought to consult the library. However, once the product was purchased, the attorneys thought the librarians should administer it. The real wake-up call came when it was time to renew the product. The contract amount almost doubled, and I was asked to put it in the library's budget for the upcoming year. The lesson I learned from this is that I needed to be more proactive in marketing the library to the specific practice group that approved this purchase. I began my marketing campaign to put the library on their radar for consultation in their search for resources by holding a training session for that group's paralegals. We also began to set up topic-specific searches for current awareness on a one-on-one basis in hopes of bringing our services to the forefront.

I also discovered that one of the practice groups was outsourcing litigation searches. This is something the library does very well, so, again, it showed me that the library was not promoting our services to the firm. I met with some paralegals from this practice group and discussed the services the library offered. They were surprised the library could perform the litigation searches they had been outsourcing. They were even more surprised to learn we could do them for much less money than the vendor.

Another marketing strategy was to use the firm's intranet to promote our services. However, I soon realized the biggest success was word of mouth. I found that attorneys listen to one another more than they read my posts on the intranet. Whenever we are given a compliment on our services, I always say, "Tell your friends!"

Another important marketing strategy is arranging face time. Because our library is spread out over nine different floors and we have sections of shelving spread out throughout the firm, we do not always get face-to-face interaction with our users. I placed importance on hand-delivering requested items instead of sending them through interoffice mail. This allowed me to see patrons on a more regular basis. In addition, we gave up our offices to be on a different floor so that we would be using the same elevator bank the attorneys use. Our reference requests have increased because we run into our users in the elevator, which reminds them we are here to help.

Along with communicating the value of the library to its users, there can also be the challenge of reporting to a top-level manager (C, or chief, level) who is not a librarian. I have been fortunate in that the executive director to whom I report understands the importance of the library. However, he knows little about the day-to-day operations of the department. In 2007, we were preparing to replace our library automation system, and he asked to be invited to the demonstration of the new system. He explained that he had seen software purchases in the past which he felt were not used to full potential, and he wanted to be sure the automated system was something we needed. After watching the first demonstration and getting a glimpse into our work flow, he was surprised by all that goes into the day-to-day operations of the library. From his level, the library was mostly Lexis and Westlaw, so this demonstration helped him gain an understanding of the other things the library does to maintain operations, keep everyone informed, and make tools our attorneys need accessible.

WHERE TO GO FOR HELP

It is possible you could end up in a position where there isn't really anyone inside the organization who can mentor or help you. In this situation, an electronic discussion list can be a great resource. This is a list for individuals with common interests, goals, and professions, with many options for delivery of content. If you are concerned about filling up your e-mail box with irrelevant messages, you can opt to have messages delivered in real time or as a digest once a day. Such lists can be invaluable for posting questions to a group of librarians who work in the same library setting as you, but they include broad groups of all kinds of librarians, even very specific groups such as catalogers in medical libraries.

Associations are another valuable source of support. Many large associations have smaller sections that cater to specific professions. For example, I am a member of AALL (American Association of Law Libraries) and, within that, a member of PLL (Private Law Libraries). There is also a chapter called SEAALL (Southeastern chapter of the American Association of Law Libraries). Chapters are designed to connect librarians geographically, with different chapters offering continuing education programs specific to the needs of their members. ALA has similar types of sections called Round Table Committees (www.ala.org/groups/committees/rts), which cover areas such as government documents, library instruction, new members, and more.

Annual meetings of library associations are wonderful opportunities to meet colleagues. If it's your first time requesting travel funds and/or work time from management, start with a regional chapter meeting instead of the larger annual meetings. Management should consider these meetings important for librarians, but this is not always the case. Since I have become a manager, my executive director, along with our human resources department, has been very supportive of sending me to the annual conference. When I return, he always asks about it, and I always have some new information to share. It is a great time for us to discuss what I've learned about emerging technologies and what other law firms are doing in their libraries. The first time I asked for permission to attend an annual conference, I gathered together all of the courses I wanted to attend and wrote a brief explanation about how each of them would benefit me and the library. The previous library manager had never attended any association meetings, so it was an eye-opener for management to see the extent of the course offerings.

Despite all of the distance learning opportunities available, nothing can replace physically attending an annual or regional association meeting. I always return energized and excited about all of the new things I've learned. The networking opportunities are limited only by how social and outgoing you may be. I am hardly an extrovert, but I find it easy to meet new people at annual meetings because we all have something in common.

Networking is critical in keeping up with the profession because no one person can know it all. At conferences I have met people I can call on for help in my daily work. At an SLA (Special Libraries Association) meeting one year, during our library catalog user group meeting, I met a librarian who worked for the Financial Accounting Standards Board and one who worked for the Federal Bureau of Investigation.

HOW DO I STAY AHEAD OF THE CURVE?

Choosing librarianship as a career means choosing a lifetime of continuing education. It can be easy to become complacent. Even if you are happy in your career and not looking to move up or to take on more responsibility, you must keep up with current and new technology to maintain your value in the workplace. When you are trying to make a change, it seems to take forever—the exact opposite of a situation in which change is "forced" upon you. The best way to prepare for future change is to be ahead of the game. Read the literature, attend the trade shows, and enroll in the occasional webinar to keep abreast of available technology. Read, read, and read more!

By virtue of being librarians, we should know how to find every tidbit of information available. Being able to find information that relates specifically to the issues librarians are facing should not be a big problem. It is important to keep reading. There is no way that anyone can keep up with all of the technology changes in the library field, let alone when you are starting from scratch. All kinds of literature, written by librarians for librarians, are available. Read general management or human resource materials that may provide ways to deal with your current situation. If you cannot find something on your topic, ask other librarians what they have read or what they recommend.

One particular publication that has proved invaluable to me is *How to Manage a Law Firm Library* from Aspatore's Inside the Minds series (Aspatore Books, 2008). The chapters, written by law firm library managers and directors, take a practical approach, including real-life examples and sample charts. Although the series is geared toward private law firms, the information could be valuable to a librarian in any setting.

The most important thing to remember when you accept a new position or new responsibilities is that you are there to make your boss look good. As long as you do that, you have nothing to worry about. Remember to be patient with yourself and open and flexible to learning opportunities. There is always something to learn about librarianship. When you find you lack the skills needed, draw on the ones you already have in order to develop the ones that you need.

WE'VE ALWAYS DONE IT THIS WAY

Katherine Farmer

One of the most challenging parts of a new job is figuring out when and how to make suggestions for changes. As a new employee, you don't want to step on your new colleagues' toes. On the other hand, continuing to do things a certain way simply because "we've always done it this way" may not make sense. This chapter looks at ways to assess your new environment and diplomatically negotiate change where needed, as well as how to recognize that some things are done certain ways for very good reasons.

MAKING YOUR MARK

Many thoughts percolated in my brain the day I started a new library position. I considered the new technologies, theories, and trends that I had encountered in graduate school, in journal articles, at workshops, and at conferences. I wondered how I could implement some of those ideas in my new position. I wanted to make my mark and show everyone what I am capable of accomplishing. I wondered, "How can I make everyone notice me as a leader and an agent of change and acknowledge what I can do? What changes can I put in place to make that happen?"

At this point I realized I needed to stop, take a breath, and think before speaking and acting about making changes at my new library. *Change* is a scary word for many people, and it is not always necessary. Any librarian in a new position should take the time to consider a few points before discussing change.

First, you have already made a big change at the library simply by accepting the position and joining an established community. You will be expected to spend time learning the position and creating working relationships with everyone, from library professionals to patrons. Both of those groups will be observing you to see how well you become part of the team, not what changes you wish to implement at the library.

Second, you may encounter direct and open resistance to any suggestions for change. This is especially true if you make them in the first week, the first month, or even the first year if you have not taken the time to build relationships, learn the history of the organization, and develop a concrete plan with input from colleagues.

My colleagues were quick to advise me when I started my new job that I should suggest changes slowly and carefully. Suggesting changes too soon can prompt your new colleagues to repeat a familiar mantra, "We have always done it this way. We don't need to change anything." If you persist at this point, you may end up with strained relationships with your colleagues. The question you must ask yourself is, "How can I suggest and implement necessary changes without overburdening my own workload and causing turmoil, rejection, and hurt feelings among my coworkers?"

INSERTING YOURSELF INTO AN ALREADY EXISTING STRUCTURE

Before you begin to initiate changes, it is critical that you understand the structure of the library and your place within that structure. The basic structure of a library involves how different positions are grouped into departments (circulation, reference, cataloging, etc.), which then function together as one library. Each department has a head who is in charge of the members of the department, and that department head reports to the library director. This departmental structure dictates how decisions are made and who makes what decisions. For example, the head of cataloging will probably make the final decisions about cataloging priorities and cataloging standards used within the library, and this person will decide whether to solicit suggestions from the cataloging staff or make the decision autonomously.

The departmental structure likewise dictates how different departments work together and who is responsible within those individual departments to work with other departments to make decisions. Usually department heads work with the library director to make final decisions that affect the entire library. They may create committees to study a problem and use the committees' recommendations to make final decisions. Department heads select representatives from within their departments to serve on committees, or they may ask for volunteers. If this opportunity presents itself, you may find it valuable to volunteer for a committee. This offers you the chance to see the corporate structure in action and to develop working relationships across departments.

For example, during my first week on the job, the chair of the marketing committee invited me to serve on the committee. I accepted and had the opportunity to work on library-wide projects that included setting up visual displays. Working on these projects allowed me to develop relationships with other professionals across the library. Building relationships can prove very helpful when you need assistance with projects or support for changes you want to implement. A few months later, I was assigned a large project to dismantle a preview collection that had been discontinued at the library. Because I had developed good working relationships with my colleagues, I knew whom to approach with questions and requests for assistance.

When discussing the structure of the library, it is important to remember that the library director sits at the top. The director's responsibilities include, but are not limited to, managing the day-to-day operations of the library and overseeing all patron services. It is the director's responsibility to initiate and approve any changes that affect the entire library and to approve any major changes at the departmental level. Minor changes at the departmental level can usually be made without the director's approval, but department heads must still inform the library director about what occurs in their departments. If you have a suggestion for change that could affect the library as a whole, you should address it with your department head instead of speaking directly to the director—or, worse, taking steps to make changes on your own. If you address the library director first instead of your department head, you ignore the structure of the library, and this can create resentment.

In my own situation, the university has a Curriculum Materials Center located at the College of Education, operated jointly by the library and the College of Education. I was assigned to serve as a liaison to the College of Education. I quickly became convinced that part of the collection was arranged in a confusing manner, making it difficult for patrons and the student worker staff to use. I developed a concrete plan for rearranging the collection before approaching the head of the Curriculum Materials Center. Because I did the necessary planning and followed protocol, the changes were approved. Had I implemented changes on my own or spoken to the upper management of the library first, it would have created a difficult working environment filled with resentment and a lack of respect.

Outside forces can also affect change at the library. In the case of a public library, the director reports to a board. The director must seek the board's approval for certain changes and decisions, especially policy decisions. For instance, if the circulation policy needs to be changed to reflect the addition of electronic books, the director drafts a new policy that reflects these additions to the collection and outlines how they will circulate to the public. The new policy, is then presented to the board for approval. The board may accept or reject the new policy, or they may ask for other revisions. Then the board approval process begins again. The board is responsible for approving the library's budget and hiring new employees. The board's actions are presented to the public and the library staff through open-door board meetings and reports to the city council.

In the case of an academic library, the library director, who is referred to as dean at some academic libraries, reports to the college president and executive members of his or her administration (e.g., provost or vice president). Other departments at the college may also have oversight of certain functions of the library. For example, the decision to hire new staff must be approved by the human resources department, which oversees the hiring process. College-wide committees, like academic council and faculty senate, may also have some oversight of library governance. Certain policy matters may require the approval of the college's board of trustees. Many changes happen behind closed doors. Consequently, library professionals do not always see the political wrangling that occurs.

Your first opportunity to learn more about the structure of your library is during the job interview. The interviewer will explain to whom you would report and if anyone would report to you. This is the basic breakdown of a localized structure within which you would work. The job announcement may also provide a detailed description of your responsibilities and areas of control. In addition, it may provide a guide to areas where it is acceptable for you consider making changes.

Another source of information about the library's structure, one that also provides detailed descriptions of job positions, is a library policies manual (public/K–12 school libraries) or library faculty handbook (academic libraries). In larger libraries, an organizational chart may be included in these documents. This information provides guidance on the channels to work within when initiating change. Each library department may also have its own manual that describes how that department functions and its policies and procedures. Spending time acquainting yourself with these documents can be valuable to understanding the structure of the library.

Observation is yet another source of information about the library structure. This begins at the interview. During your tour of the library, you may see professionals working and communicating with one another. While these observations cannot always be counted on to portray an accurate picture since people may be putting on a good face, they are a starting point. During your first week at your new position, observe how different library professionals interact with one another. Through these observations, you will discover the best ways to interact with your colleagues on a daily basis within the library's structure.

Armed with what you have learned about the library's structure, use the first week or two to get to know your colleagues. You might even choose to spend time with them outside of the library walls since people are more likely to converse with you if you show an interest in them and present yourself in a friendly manner. At this point, you can ask questions about what they are working on now and how you could assist with their projects. A word of warning: remember that you are asking to help with their project, not to take over the project; you will harm any relationships you are trying to build by appearing too controlling.

During my first week at my new library position, I reacquainted myself with the staff. Every time I encountered a new colleague, I took the time to introduce myself again. During those first few weeks, I also ate lunch with different library groups. Be careful to avoid making assumptions when getting to know the library's structure and your new colleagues. For instance, don't assume that a library professional will resist change just because he or she has worked at the library most of his or her career. Instead, take the time to understand why things are done a certain way. By listening to your colleagues' perspectives, you will foster an atmosphere of respect instead of negative resistance.

FINDING OUT WHICH THINGS ARE DONE A CERTAIN WAY

As a new librarian, you are expected to ask an abundance of questions. In fact, you should use this time to ask specific questions about why certain things are done a certain way. You may be surprised by what you discover (hint: old may not be bad). Your colleagues will probably be glad to explain the rationale for decisions. They want you to respect the process and history that existed before you came to the library. Rather than finding that your new colleagues have shied away from change, you may discover that they have tried or explored several different methods of accomplishing a task. Through trial and error, they may have concluded that the old way works best for the library and its patrons. Once you know why certain decisions were made, you may realize that the old way is perfect and change is not necessary.

During my first four months at the library and with the Curriculum Materials Center, I devoted time to learning the history of the center, how it was organized, and the reasons behind decisions. By taking the time to learn the history, I was able to avoid mistakes, to carefully develop relationships with the patrons and faculty, to thoughtfully plan any changes, and to be considerate of the way things had always been done. For example, some materials at the Curriculum Materials Center had been specifically placed in the collection by current faculty members. Due to the worn condition of the materials, I questioned whether the items should be retained. After I learned the history of the Curriculum Materials Center and these materials, I worked with the faculty to decide whether to weed certain items. Had I followed my first inclination and weeded the items myself, I would have offended my colleagues and created a sense of mistrust. Bear in mind that once you have created such feelings, it can be very difficult to undo them. Instead, I created a positive working environment because I demonstrated respect for the head of the Curriculum Materials Center and for other colleagues' contributions to the library.

Another way to learn why things are done a certain way is to read about the library. If the library has existed for more than fifty years, someone may have compiled its history. Large libraries have policy manuals for various areas of the library; small libraries will probably have a single policy manual. If you work at a public library, board minutes may be available. As more and more information becomes available digitally, you may find other meeting minutes stored on a shared drive or in an employee-only wiki. Some libraries have ventured into social media through Facebook, Twitter, and blogs. These can provide insight into happenings at the library and possibly the public's opinion of the library. As you read this material, try to understand how and why your colleagues created certain policy decisions.

If you are part of the public face of the library, start to build relationships with the patrons. They may tell you how they see the library operating and whether change is needed. This may arise through casual conversation or by asking the simple question "Did you find everything that you needed?" If your library has a Friends of the Library organization, learn its history and meet the members. They have a vested interest in the library and may also have insight into changes that the public might wish to see.

KNOWING WHEN AND HOW TO MAKE SUGGESTIONS FOR RATIONAL CHANGE

Change in any organization, especially a large organization, can take time. After coming to an understanding of the organizational structure of the library, safely integrating yourself into the structure, and examining the operational and organizational history of the library, you should have concluded that change does not happen overnight. Small changes, like how to organize a department's work flow, may happen in a matter of weeks. Larger changes, like those to the library's circulation policy, may require months to enact.

In spite of all the considerations mentioned, you may still see the need for changes. Before you open the office door to engage your colleagues in a discussion, consider the following points.

It can be tricky to find the right moment to make suggestions for change. Making suggestions during the first week, unless specifically asked, is paramount to disaster. The library staff will think that you are trying to take over and that you do not appreciate what was done before you came. For example, a new librarian at my library who accepted a position that had been vacant for some time did not consult the staff who had operated the department before she developed a plan for change. When she presented the information and changes to the staff, she did not consider their points of view or show appreciation for their previous work. The staff felt hurt and unappreciated and openly resisted her changes. The new librarian realized her mistake and had to immediately start repairing relationships.

Before making unsolicited suggestions, analyze the situation and develop concrete reasons for any changes. Research the problem in light of the library's history, current trends, and the actions of other libraries before presenting suggestions to colleagues. This demonstrates that you devoted time to careful consideration.

> ## Tips for Initiating Change
>
> ❖ Find the right moment to introduce change.
>
> ❖ Analyze the situation and develop concrete reasons for change.
>
> ❖ Discover the library's tolerance for change through conversations with colleagues and by reflecting on projects already started.
>
> ❖ Make clearly stated suggestions for change and include a timeline.
>
> ❖ Allow colleagues to assist in developing changes.
>
> ❖ Keep the library's organizational structure in mind when suggesting change.
>
> ❖ Start small.

When I was working with an established colleague at the Curriculum Materials Center, I noticed that the center's acquisitions process was cumbersome, time consuming, and haphazard. This often caused patrons' needs to go unmet. Understanding that a change needed to take place, I studied the situation from all angles, politely questioned the seasoned professional about the history of the current process, asked other library professionals for advice, and developed a new acquisitions process for the center. With a well-developed plan in hand, I was able to change the way the Curriculum Materials Center handled the acquisition process to better meet the patrons' needs.

Another factor that guides the decision of when to make a change is the library's overall atmosphere. With new technology and budget crunches, library staff may already feel overwhelmed by constant change. Staff may reject additional changes in order to regroup mentally and to catch up on other responsibilities. At other times, the atmosphere of the library may feel stagnant, and the library staff may accept suggestions for change as a breath of fresh air. The library's tolerance level for change can be judged through conversations with colleagues and by reflecting on projects already under way.

Consider certain factors when presenting change to your colleagues. First, make sure your suggestions are clearly stated and easily understood. For example, instead of simply stating that the circulation policy needs to be altered, explain that it needs to be updated to reflect the addition of electronic books to the collection. Second, include a timeline of how long it will take to implement the change. In terms of the circulation policy, you could state that the library will need to spend approximately one day to update the circulation policy to include electronic books. Finally, include information that helps your colleagues see the need for the change and explains how they can assist with the process.

After creating the proposal, examine the procedures for how things will be accomplished. Recognition of these procedures, or the proverbial red tape, should be included in your proposal to your supervisors, the head of the department, or the library director. Failure to consider potential roadblocks can cause your initiative to stall or fall flat.

Allowing your colleagues to assist with the development of a change and its implementation removes the atmosphere of negativity from the library. Negativity can derail improvements if the staff do not feel that they are part of the process. On the other hand, if the staff feel they are stakeholders, the project has a greater chance of succeeding.

Always keep the library's organizational structure in mind when suggesting changes. If you are a member of the cataloging department and have a suggestion for a better way to catalog media items, the proper procedure would be to talk with your department head rather than taking the matter to the library director. This can avoid creating tense relationships.

Sometimes, however, following the chain of command does not work. Your department head may be too busy to entertain your suggestions. If this is the case, you may decide to address the situation with the library director or another department head. If you take this route, be up front with your department head. Your department head may be pleased that you handled the situation. In my own experience, a faculty member at my university approached me about a project to create a display of local artifacts. She specifically requested assistance in developing the exhibit with artifacts from the library's archives. I contacted a colleague who could help her with the project. After setting up the meeting, I spoke to my director and apologized if I had overstepped my authority. In this case, he was glad that I had handled the situation. However, you may not always be so lucky when you act outside the established protocol.

Finally, start with small changes. These can build over time to create a major change at the library. As a point of consideration, you could break down any major project into smaller pieces so that the change will not appear threatening and overwhelming. Prioritizing small changes is key to making sure the project is realized successfully.

TAKING RESPONSIBILITY FOR MISTAKES

Just because you plan carefully does not mean you will not make mistakes or push too hard. When you make a mistake (and you will, just as I have and every librarian before you has), take a moment to think before you react. The first reaction can be worse than the actual mistake. Don't become defensive and refuse to listen to others. If you listen to others, you may discover there is an easy solution. For example, one day the library printer was malfunctioning, and the daily statistics did not print. The librarian who printed the statistics did not realize the printer was not working properly. When she was told, she became angry and did not listen to how to fix the problem. The result was that it took thirty minutes instead of five to fix the problem.

Take responsibility when you make a mistake. Denying responsibility or blaming others will likely make things worse. Your colleagues will respect you more for owning up to your mistakes and working to correct them. They will distance themselves from you if they think you will blame them for your mistakes.

Finally, there will be instances when your colleagues feel pushed too hard to make changes. Pay attention to their tone of voice and body language and to the general atmosphere of the library. When it becomes apparent that you need to slow things down, don't be afraid to adjust deadlines or to break the project into smaller pieces. One spring, a committee was formed at my library to rewrite the collection development policy to account for new material types and policy changes. Almost immediately after the first meeting, the library received a donation to renovate the reference room. The renovation project had to begin immediately in order to be completed before classes started in the fall. The committee postponed the rewriting of the collection development policy until the fall because the staff felt too overwhelmed to write a collection development policy as well as plan and assist with the renovation.

FINAL THOUGHTS

As you enter this new phase of your library career, don't be afraid of change or be discouraged by a lack of encouragement, as these will come eventually. Change is a sign that libraries evolve as society evolves. Libraries exist to serve the needs of their patrons and libraries must change as patrons' needs change. Remember that the old ways of doing things are not always bad and that tactful ways to introduce change do exist.

PROFESSIONAL ASSOCIATIONS AND YOU

Lynda Kellam

There are many professional associations and organizations that librarians can join. Should you? Is there a payback? If so, how do you find your niche? This chapter explores the rewards, as well as the challenges and obligations of joining professional organizations. It offers strategies for reaping the most benefits and gives insight from leaders in the field. This chapter also explores the path of involvement in professional associations, from choosing one to join, to finding a niche in the organization, to moving up into leadership positions.

HOW DO I FIND A PROFESSIONAL HOME?

Involvement in professional associations is an integral component of the profession for many librarians. The moment we enter library school, we begin receiving offers to join the American Library Association or state library associations. We start searching for our niche within these large impersonal organizations, and we volunteer for committee assignments as soon as we accept our first professional positions. As we progress through our careers, we may also progress through the ranks of leadership within these professional associations. How do we find our homes within professional library associations? How do we ensure that our participation is successful? How do we move up the ladder once we have found an entry point?

Some librarians are eager to jump into professional activity and find it enjoyable; others question the purpose or hesitate to join an unknown organization. Yet involvement can be crucial to your development as a professional. Are there ways to

> ## I Chose the Following Interviewees to Ensure a Balanced Distribution of Leaders in Different Types of Library Organizations:
>
> - Pete Bromberg (America Library Association and Learning Round Table)
> - Buffy Hamilton (American Association of School Librarians and Georgia Library Media Association)
> - Mary Krautter (Special Libraries Association and the Kentucky Chapter of the Special Libraries Association)
> - Lauren Pressley (American Library Association and ALA Council)

become more immersed in an organization and to be strategic about moving into leadership positions? Librarians who are leaders in a variety of professional organizations believe so and offer snippets of wisdom. This chapter assumes that professional involvement can benefit any librarian's career. It has benefitted mine.

JOINING IS FOR JOINERS—WHY SHOULD I?

Why should you get involved with professional organizations? Some librarians are incredulous that anyone would fail to see the benefits. However, a growing number of new librarians appear skeptical about joining, especially when factoring in the expense of dues, conferences, and other costs. In addition, some new librarians feel intimidated by the size of organizations like the American Library Association (ALA), which has more than sixty thousand members. Others want to join the most appropriate organizations for their careers but do not know which ones are good matches. In instances where a librarian is the only one in a particular position, it can be even more difficult to identify appropriate associations because there may not be anyone who can make recommendations.

While the expense of involvement may seem prohibitive, remember that joining and working with an organization helps spread your name among colleagues who may be in a position to hire you or to inform you about upcoming job opportunities. It is not necessary to attend every conference to learn about opportunities or to get your name into the mix. All organizations have electronic mailing lists or social networking sites where you can mingle virtually. There can be a great benefit to having ready-made connections.

Moreover, professional involvement demonstrates a commitment to librarianship that goes beyond a monthly paycheck. Joining an association and volunteering your time shows potential colleagues and employers that you are interested in engaging with the profession and its future. Whether you are a student, job seeker, or first-year professional looking to move up, becoming involved in professional organizations can provide a forum for both learning and self-promotion. Pete Bromberg, Assistant Director of the Princeton Public Library, ranked networking as "one of the greatest benefits" of joining a professional organization. He notes that it provides "the opportunity for mutual inspiration and learning" through relationships with smart, creative, and generous colleagues from all types of libraries.

This network is indispensable not only for getting ahead but also for doing your job. In my work as a data librarian, I have sometimes needed help from other data librarians to answer patrons' questions. My home state has very few librarians with data expertise, but my membership in the International Association for Social Science Information Services and Technology (IASSIST) gives me access to colleagues all over the world. For example, when I needed to track down historical statistics about New Zealand that were unavailable in our print and electronic sources, I contacted a colleague working for Statistics New Zealand.

In addition to being a resource, the network offers excellent informal and formal mentoring opportunities, both in person and virtual. It is invaluable for a new librarian to have someone outside the workplace who can provide open and honest feedback. Since this person doesn't supervise you, there isn't as much pressure in his or her comments. Of course, these connections can be made outside of professional associations, but associations provide convenient conduits. Even if an association does not have a formal program in place, you can use your networking skills to find someone. You could even help create a mentoring program, which would be a great way to make your name known! Within ALA, the New Members Round Table (NMRT) provides two formal programs: a conference mentoring program and a professional career mentoring program. Both are great places to find someone who is a good fit for your career goals. Buffy Hamilton, former high school librarian and teacher at The Unquiet Library in Canton, Georgia, noted that the opportunity to network allowed her to "learn from so many wise colleagues across my state and across the country. Not only does getting involved allow you to serve your organization, but it also provides you a medium for forming partnerships for learning with other library professionals who can help you problem solve and improve your practice."

Don't wait until you have a "real" job before joining an association. Students receive excellent rates on membership and conference registration. If you join as a student, you can establish your network early and gain contacts for your job search. Even if you are not able to travel to conferences, once you have a network of people or have discovered your "role" in an association, you can serve virtually. This will help you feel more connected during years when you cannot actively participate. It will also help keep your name in front of others.

Some Professional Organizations to Consider Joining

- American Library Association (ALA), www.ala.org: ALA was created to provide leadership for the development, promotion, and improvement of library and information services and the profession of librarianship.

- Association for Information Science and Technology (ASIS&T), www.asis.org: ASIS&T advances the information sciences and related applications of information technology by providing focus, opportunity, and support to information professionals and organizations.

- Association of Research Libraries (ARL), www.arl.org: ARL influences the changing environment of scholarly communication and the public policies that affect research libraries and the diverse communities they serve.

- Coalition for Networked Information (CNI), www.cni.org: CNI is an organization dedicated to supporting the transformative promise of digital information technology for the advancement of scholarly communication and the enrichment of intellectual productivity.

- International Federation of Library Associations and Institutions (IFLA), www.ifla.org: IFLA is the leading international body representing the interests of library and information services and their users.

- North American Serials Interest Group (NASIG), www.nasig.org: NASIG is an independent organization that promotes communication and sharing of ideas among all members of the serials information chain—anyone working with or concerned about serial publications.

- Society of American Archivists (SAA), http://www2.archivists.org: SAA serves the educational and informational needs of its members and provides leadership to ensure the identification, preservation, and use of records of historical value.

BUT THERE ARE SO MANY—WHERE DO I GO?

The first step in deciding what to join is to think critically about which organizations or divisions within an organization would benefit you most and what level of organization (state or national) would be most feasible for you. Ask other librarians who do similar work for suggestions.

Pete Bromberg recommends that all new librarians join ALA's NMRT (New Members Round Table). If the new librarian already has a clearly defined role or interest, he suggests seeking out the specific unit within ALA (division, round table, special interest group) aligned with that interest. He further suggests reaching out to the membership of that unit, attending meetings when possible, and offering to help with projects/initiatives. He stresses that making offers to help is *always* a good way to get involved, and he predicts it won't be long before leadership opportunities present themselves. New librarians who are less clear on their focus can explore the ALA website and ALA Connect to identify potential choices. Bromberg advises, "ALA Connect is an excellent way to become involved. Or pick up the phone and call leaders of ALA units and ask them if they can give you ten to fifteen minutes of their time to explain what their unit is all about. If you have a chance to go to conference, be an inveterate sampler of meetings and programs, introduce yourself to everyone, and make offers to help with anything that inspires you."

In addition to following your own interests, your library administration may expect you to belong to a certain division in ALA. For example, most government information librarians are expected to join the Government Documents Round Table (GODORT). Most academic librarians are expected to join the Association of College and Research Libraries (ACRL). Joining each of these divisions costs money, so always consider what is best for you. If you think your time and energy can be better spent in another association, explain to your library director or supervisor why your chosen association is a better fit.

Also consider the level at which you would like to spend most of your time. Would you prefer national, regional, or state? Librarians in niche positions may need to focus their energies in national or international organizations. Lauren Pressley, instructional design librarian at Wake Forest University in North Carolina, chose to focus primarily on a national organization, ALA. Since few people in her state do the kind of work she does, she decided it made more sense for her to work at the national level. She also likes working with a national organization because she likes the idea of contributing to work that will impact the field as a whole.

On the other hand, some state organizations are well organized and active, and your supervisor may expect work at that level. Typically, a major benefit of state-level work is the ability to gain committee membership and leadership experience quickly. In my first month of employment, I was asked to run for a leadership position within a subdivision of our state organization. State-level organizations also provide a network of colleagues who share similar challenges and opportunities. Meeting them can make you feel more connected within the state and also help sharpen the skills you will need to serve effectively at the national level. Service at the state level will also give you an opportunity to learn the structure of associations or "how things work."

While ALA is the primary organization for librarians, other organizations may also be a good match. For example, IASSIST serves the data professionals' population, but it is not primarily an organization of librarians. EDUCAUSE is popular with librarians interested in technology issues, but, again, it is not primarily an organization of librarians. There are many possibilities with organizations from other fields. For example, joining a subject area professional organization, such as the Modern Language Association for humanities librarians or the American Political Science Association for political science librarians, may be especially helpful for subject specialist librarians. In her 2011 article "The Benefits of Non-library Professional Organization Membership for Liaison Librarians" (*The Journal of Academic Librarianship* 37, no. 1: 46–53), Miranda Bennett notes that membership in nonlibrary organizations helps build awareness of subject areas and builds bridges between subject experts and librarians. Membership demonstrates to the subject experts that librarians are interested in and committed to the future of their field. Organizations outside of the library field may be especially useful if you are in a unique position. Be creative in thinking about associations that might provide you with useful information in your field as well as give you access to others who do similar work.

There is no one path to finding a niche. Lauren Pressley began her involvement with ALA as a member of the Committee on the Status of Women in Librarianship (COSWL). She threw her name into the volunteer process as a library school student, expecting it to take a few tries before getting appointed. She chose COSWL because she had a background in women's studies and thought it would be a nice connection between her academic and professional interests. To her surprise, she ended up getting a spot on the committee. She also wanted to be involved with ALA's Library and Information Technology Association (LITA) for the technology side of her interests, so she sat in on a Distance Learning Interest Group meeting at an ALA conference. There she volunteered to help set up a wiki for the group, which cemented her working relationship with that group for years to come.

I JOINED—NOW WHAT?

You have filled out the form, sent off your check, and are now a card-carrying member of a professional association. What's next? How do you become more than a name in the "Welcome!" section of the organization's newsletter? How do you get involved in a meaningful way? How do you move up into a leadership position?

The first step is to volunteer for a committee or a special project. While on a committee, you can offer to complete a task or propose ideas. The point is to demonstrate your interest in the committee's work in a productive manner and to contribute to the life of the committee. Lauren Pressley started out in ALA by volunteering for COSWL and the Instruction Committee of the Women's Studies Section of ACRL. Buffy Hamilton recommends volunteering for roles or responsibilities that challenge you and help you grow or that build on talents which will help you contribute to the organization. She became active in the American Association of School Librarians (AASL) by volunteering to serve on governing committees within the association. The experience of being involved in different areas of an association allows a new member to gain the confidence, perspective, and skills needed to help listen as well as lead.

The skill of listening can be critical in the early years of your committee work. While it is fine to offer ideas, don't be overly insistent or offer too many ideas. This might give the impression you are trying to take over and may cause people to tune you out. Listening carefully also gives you a more nuanced understanding of some of the issues the committee is dealing with.

Volunteering is one thing, but follow-through is critical. If you volunteer for a committee assignment or a special project, you must be willing and have the time to follow through with your commitment. We all have months (or years) when we are overloaded, have volunteered ourselves too widely, and may not be able to contribute 100 percent to a project. If you become overloaded, it is best to communicate with colleagues and other committee members. Ask a colleague in your library to give you some relief by helping with your work duties, such as taking your desk time or teaching one of your classes. Other committee members may be willing to help with an assignment or project for which you volunteered. The key is to be honest with yourself, your colleagues, and your committee members when you recognize that you are overloaded. It is even better to avoid those walls before you run into them. Learning when to say no is a valuable skill.

At the same time, remember to sometimes say yes. If you consistently reject offers, your name will be removed from lists. You do not want to be passed up for a coveted opportunity because you never volunteered for smaller duties. Find your balance, but show yourself to be an engaged and productive member of a committee.

Just as you need to think strategically about which umbrella organization to join, you also need to think strategically about committees or sections. All umbrella associations, ALA or state, have smaller committees or sections. Some of these are extremely large, like ACRL, while others are small. Unless a popular committee is your dream appointment, start in smaller or less popular sections and work your way into the appointments you really want.

For example, the Information Literacy Section of ACRL is very large and extremely popular with instruction librarians. It may take time and effort to become a committee member. In contrast, the subject-specific sections are generally begging for volunteers and committee members. An instruction librarian with an interest in political science or public policy could gain tremendous leadership experience in a smaller group, such as ACRL's Law and Political Science Section. If your supervisor questions your choice of focus, explain that the smaller group will help you gain leadership and teamwork skills and ultimately improve your chances of joining a committee in a larger section.

While the state-level committees may have fewer members and provide more opportunities for leadership, you could still be active in a group at the national level. Leadership in a state-level organization will give you the skills and positions on your résumé necessary to then make your way into national leadership. This may also be true for other innovative services or projects you would like to try. National-level sections tend to have larger bureaucracies than state-level associations and may not provide as much room for innovation. A state association may allow you to accomplish new projects, providing proof of concept for possible innovations at the national level.

Finally, the current leaders of your chosen section will eventually move up or move on to new positions or even retire. If you have your foot in the door, you are in a much better place to move into a leadership position. Look for these opportunities and consider carefully what matches your interests, abilities, and needs.

Lauren Pressley knew she wanted to work with ALA governance, but she thought it would be a long time before that happened. However, the nomination committee was looking for new members to nominate for council that year, and she was approached to run. Her mentors pointed out that it usually takes a few runs to get elected, so she threw her hat into the ring. Once she was running, she let people know she was interested. She set up a website with a video explaining her interest. She doesn't know that it made a difference, but the video got a lot of hits, particularly around election time.

She ended up focusing on ALA's LITA because she wanted to spend time working for a group where her contribution would have an impact. She believed that LITA was small enough for one person to make a real difference. She also wanted to work with an agile group that could model new ways of thinking for associations for ALA.

Mary Krautter, Head of Reference at the University of North Carolina at Greensboro, notes that it's a necessity to have some involvement outside one's own library in order to maintain knowledge of new trends and to gain new skills. The new ideas learned at professional conferences can bring value to your own job. "Anyone who becomes too insulated can become stale and resistant to change. You can also expand your professional network and find colleagues who can be useful to you in many ways, as well as friends who will support you professionally and personally. Also, learning to work in a variety of group settings is an invaluable lesson. Each organization and each group within an organization has its own dynamics. Learning to negotiate within a variety of settings is a needed skill that is universally applicable. Becoming a leader allows one to develop one's own leadership style and to become more confident in presenting ideas within any setting."

BUT CAN I MEET THE CHALLENGES?

In addition to the benefits, there can also be challenges to joining organizations. The first challenge is time. You have to decide how that time can be balanced with your current life situation as well as your regular work duties. Pete Bromberg points out that getting involved with ALA might seem daunting to new librarians, but he encourages them to embrace being a little overwhelmed in the short term. He notes that the long-term payoff to one's enrichment and satisfaction as a librarian is a hundredfold. What you learn and the relationships you form through association activity will benefit you throughout your career.

A second challenge is that professional involvement costs money. Except in special cases, you will have to pay dues, and these can add up over time. Moreover, each individual conference includes registration fees and travel expenses. Your workplace may pay for all or part of these, but funding may not always be available. You may be required to pay some out-of-pocket expenses. You must decide if these are expenses you can afford to bear. Consider how your professional involvement balances with your life priorities and whether you are able to invest the time and money required. Be strategic about where your time and your money can be best spent.

Mary Krautter found travel funding a primary drawback. She has often funded her own professional development, and she sometimes finds it challenging to balance time commitments at work with broader professional leadership roles.

Pete Bromberg finds a major drawback is that there are so many opportunities to contribute to and be involved in that it can be hard to focus your energies in one place. He also points out that the bureaucracy of large organizations can be frustrating, although he thinks ALA has made great strides (e.g., with ALA Connect, Networking Uncommons, Grassroots Program) in providing members the tools and platforms to form communities, connect, and share without so much red tape.

Buffy Hamilton's biggest challenge is juggling commitments—the time commitment ebbs and flows. She deals with this by scheduling time to meet deadlines and carving out time for the work she needs to do for these organizations. Lauren Pressley also found time a challenge. Like everyone else, her job itself already takes a lot of time. Then there are the pulls of family and life outside of work. She sometimes has trouble finding where to fit professionally related nonjob work. She used to treat her professional involvement as a hobby. Now she is in a different life phase; instead of work expanding to fill all available time, she has to carve out time for it. She tries to tack on fifteen to thirty minutes a day at work for professional activities. Sometimes she just mulls over ideas in the back of her head for a few days before she has the time to act on them.

I'M IN IT FOR THE LOVE—WHAT ABOUT YOU?

Professional involvement may be purely strategic for purposes of reappointment or employment. This is perfectly understandable considering the current market and economic situation. However, it is usually obvious when someone is professionally involved for love and when someone is doing it "just for now." The last element of succeeding in professional organizations involves an intangible quality.

Lauren Pressley writes, "I love my day job, but professional work outside of the day-to-day is what I often find most rewarding." Connecting with people all over the country, doing similar work with similar goals and missions, can add a level of meaning to work that changes it from a job to a profession. For Buffy Hamilton, "being able to be part of the changes you want to see in an organization and to be an active team player is truly gratifying." Mary Krautter mentions developing a treasured friendship with someone who recently passed away. The friendship was invaluable to Mary as she learned a lot about professionalism and dedication. These are the intangibles of professional involvement—the excitement, the enrichment, the engagement. You can work on projects and serve on a committee, but if you do not have enthusiasm, what is the point? People who do it for love are the ones who will be the leaders in the future.

LIFE CYCLE OF A LIBRARIAN'S YEAR

Jenny Dale

Almost every librarian's work life is driven by some type of annual cycle. College and university libraries are tied to the academic calendar and public libraries are often tied to the school day and year. Special libraries are also subject to their own ebbs and flows. Knowing when to anticipate busy cycles and understanding how to manage your time to accommodate these cycles can make you more efficient. It can also ease your level of stress when things are at their busiest. This chapter addresses the cyclical nature of a librarian's work year and offers suggestions on how to make those cycles work for you.

WHERE DOES THE TIME GO?

My biggest challenge when I started my first librarian position was not the transition from student to professional or even the move across the country. My greatest challenge those first few months was gaining an understanding of the patterns and rhythms of my new position. I was a brand-new librarian in a brand-new position. I had no idea how to plan for the year ahead. Fortunately, I had an excellent supervisor and great colleagues who helped me shape my first year in a way that gave me solid footing for subsequent years. However, I have never forgotten how lost I felt when I began.

The more time you spend in your position, the more comfortable you are likely to become with the ebbs and flows in your workload. It takes time to identify the changes in your workload. Often there are not dramatic shifts, but instead one type of work phases into another type. For instance, after the teaching crunch at the beginning of every semester, classes taper off, and you may find yourself easing into the next phase of collection development. Often, you won't have a true sense of patterns in your workload until you have been in your position for a full year or more. In academic settings (K–12 and higher education), patterns are usually linked to the academic calendar. However, even that can change drastically if your institution is undergoing accreditation or undertaking some other major initiative. Public librarians, on the other hand, may find their workload change is seasonal. These are broad generalizations, and your experience will vary depending on your workplace, position, and personal work style. In any position, there are ways to identify and effectively respond to annual workload patterns.

Knowing how you spend your time is a critical first step to identifying workload patterns. Time studies, while sometimes tedious, can be useful exercises to help you document your time and eventually evaluate changes in your personal workload. Time studies, including time logs, help people identify how long they devote to specific tasks and responsibilities. They are also effective ways to detect avoidable interruptions and time wasters. You may discover that your workload is not overwhelming, but that you need to adopt some different strategies for managing your

Acknowledgment

While writing this chapter, I consulted several librarians whose help was invaluable to me in getting different perspectives on this topic, and I'd like to take this opportunity to thank each of them:

- Jessica C. S. Brewer
  (Librarian, Charlotte Mecklenburg Library)

- Anna Craft
  (Metadata Cataloger, UNC Greensboro University Libraries)

- Dayna Durbin
  (Library Media Coordinator, W.G. Pearson Middle School)

- Amy Harris Houk
  (Information Literacy Program Coordinator, UNC Greensboro University Libraries)

- Kim Whittington
  (Librarian, Charlotte Mecklenburg Library)

time. Isolating those periods when you are not productive is the first step to correcting the problem.

Typically, time studies are short term, taking place over the course of a week or two, or at random points in a given period. The library literature is filled with studies that make use of this traditional productivity exercise to document and explore the nature of librarians' work. An understanding of some of these studies may help you when starting a new job. Even though the focus of this chapter is a view over the long term—which can't be determined by tracking time for a week or a few representative days—tracking your time on a smaller scale is an important first step. Unless your supervisor or administration requires time analysis, it is a personal exercise, and its success depends on finding the method most useful and comfortable for you.

Time Analysis Studies

Ferguson and Taylor[1] asked seventeen academic librarians to provide detailed accounts of their time on five randomly selected workdays in a six-week period in order to analyze and classify their various work activities. Hitchingham[2] put together a snapshot of the work being done by librarians at her institution by collecting and analyzing time logs her colleagues completed.

Brown[3] kept a daily time log for seven years, tracking each activity and noting the amount of time each took. She originally intended the study to help her organize and manage her time as she worked toward tenure, but she found that her logs also allowed her to track time allocation changes over the years. Most important for our purposes, she notes, "This information allows me to take on responsibilities with a fairly accurate idea of the impact on time allocation, and to attempt to maintain a balance amongst all the responsibilities of the position" (p. 65).

1. Anthony W. Ferguson and John R. Taylor, "'What *Are* You Doing?' An Analysis of Activities of Public Service Librarians at a Medium-sized Research Library," *Journal of Academic Librarianship* 6, no. 1 (1980): 24–29.

2. Eileen E. Hitchingham, "Academic Librarians' Workload," in *Energies for Transition: Proceedings of the Fourth National Conference of the Association of College and Research Libraries, Baltimore, Maryland, April 9–12, 1986,* ed. Danuta A. Nitecki (Chicago: Association of College and Research Libraries), 133–38.

3. Jeanne M. Brown, "Time and the Academic Librarian," *portal: Libraries and the Academy* 1, no. 1 (2001): 59–70, doi: 10.1353/pla.2001.0009.

A method that has been effective for me has been to keep a continuous calendar document titled "What I did today." I try to update it daily, adding brief notes about what I accomplished that day with simple notations like "ENG 101 instruction session, search committee meeting, reference desk shift." This low level of detail works for me, as I tend to forget to record my time in small increments, making traditional time tracking a frustrating and ultimately fruitless endeavor. Over several months, I have been able to pull out patterns in my workload. These patterns have been critical to me for planning and scheduling. For instance, in September and October, I may teach fifteen library instruction sessions in a week. That leaves me little time to take on additional projects. If a writing or service opportunity arises that will require substantial work during those months, I know I must defer the opportunity or turn it down altogether if it has a set timeline. While it is sometimes disappointing to have to reject opportunities, it is far better to be realistic about what can be accomplished than to accept an obligation I cannot fulfill.

Again, keeping track of your time and your tasks is an individual process. If a method like mine isn't thorough enough to work for you, try a more detailed time log. There are many examples available. At the time of this writing, a Google search for *"time log"* brings back approximately 1.8 trillion hits. You can download spreadsheets and printable PDFs, find online document templates, or check out web-based time-tracking tools. Low-tech paper calendars can be just as effective for tracking your time in small increments, but they can be more difficult to analyze for patterns over time. Whatever method you choose, be sure that it is sustainable. Otherwise, teasing out these patterns in your workload will be nearly impossible, and you will simply have a collection of papers that hold little value for you.

IDENTIFYING PATTERNS

While no two librarians' workload cycles are alike, patterns tend to emerge among professionals in similar settings and with similar positions. This section explores the patterns that may emerge as you look at how you spend your time. Along with tasks that are clearly work related, be aware of the nonessential tasks you are performing.

Academic Librarians

As I mentioned earlier, academic librarians (for our purposes, librarians who work in institutions of higher education) often notice patterns that are closely related to the academic cycle. In my current position as an instruction librarian with reference and departmental liaison responsibilities, I find that I am busiest early in the semester and midsemester. My heaviest teaching loads occur in September and October, with February and March coming in a close second. Other instruction librarian colleagues notice similar patterns. If you are an academic librarian with a primarily public service role, it pays to get to know the patterns at your particular institution. Some professors don't bring their students over early in the semester but much later. This can significantly shift your work pattern.

While it is good to have an understanding of the work patterns at your institution, noting your personal workload changes is the best way to identify trends and patterns over time. When you are new in a position or library, ask colleagues who have been around for a few years if they have noticed trends in their workload. Depending on your institution, you may find that public service librarians are busiest with reference work during the first several weeks of the semester when there are a lot of directional and printing questions from students new to the campus. Library instructional teaching loads will also increase. Another busy time can be around the midpoint of the semester, as students prepare for midterm papers and exams. The final weeks of the semester might also be a peak time for similar reasons. A colleague at my library recently noticed a surge in class and individual research consultation requests somewhere between the middle and end of the semester. She learned that this was becoming a "second midterm" cycle for her departments.

Your workload may also be affected if you have promoted your services or if you have done a lot of outreach to your liaison departments. This may create an increase in the number of questions from faculty and students as well as an increase in requests for library instruction. Also, if a faculty member is involved in some significant research, you may start to receive in-depth and time-consuming questions.

One important thing that I have learned over the course of my career is that a busy academic library does not necessarily mean a busy librarian. The past four academic libraries where I worked were filled with students during final exam periods, but the reference desk was not busier than usual. Students are often beyond research at this point in the semester. They are spending their time in the library studying or putting final touches on papers. In my library, we still get plenty of questions during this time of the semester, but the content shifts. For instance, we see an increase in citation and formatting questions. These can sometimes be time consuming and also require a shift in thinking from research. The summer tends to be quieter, making it an opportune moment to budget time for updating LibGuides, Blackboard or Moodle modules, or other study materials.

Academic librarians with positions that are more behind the scenes may not be as closely tied to the academic year. Colleagues in technical services tell me that their workload changes are based on acquisition cycles. If your new job is as an acquisitions librarian, you may notice an increase in your workload at the beginning of the fiscal year when selectors begin to submit orders for new materials. The ordering deadline for the fiscal year is likely to be another peak in workload. As a liaison who has been known to spend a large percent of my collection budgets on the absolute last day of the acquisitions cycle, I can attest to that. Catalogers, who deal with these ordered materials when they actually arrive, will notice a different pattern, though one that is still closely tied to the acquisitions cycle. Archivists and special collections librarians may find that the patterns in their workloads are less predictable. This area tends to be heavily project driven, with workloads increasing significantly following the donation of a new collection or the awarding of a new grant. Major changes to websites and other systems tend to be saved for summer to reduce the impact on students and faculty. This means librarians whose work is technology focused may notice an increase in work during the summer, when many other academic librarians are having the opposite experience.

Depending on your institution, you may also need to factor in issues related to tenure and promotion. If you are a tenure-track librarian, it is critical to set aside time to devote to research and service activities. Again, ask a colleague—either one who is also on the tenure track or one who is already tenured—for advice on meeting tenure milestones while dealing with the day-to-day work of being a librarian. It can be easy to get caught up in the work flow, believing that you have a lot of time later to focus on tenure requirements. However, if you do not schedule time to work on your tenure package in your early work years, you may find trying to fulfill the requirements in the last year or so quite overwhelming.

Public Librarians

While public libraries aren't officially tied to an academic calendar, the public librarians I consulted while writing this chapter noted a close relationship between public school calendars and their workloads. Public service librarians in public libraries are often busier during the evenings and on weekends during the school year and all summer long. Public libraries may also be more affected by social or economic changes in the community. Public libraries provide free access to the Internet for the general public, a service that has garnered media attention in recent years. In the aftermath of Hurricane Katrina, for instance, public libraries reported an increase in use by evacuees needing government aid or simply trying to communicate with loved ones. In a down economy, free Internet access becomes even more attractive, especially for job seekers. This can result in more requests for help by patrons who are not as computer savvy.

Unlike their academic library colleagues, for public service librarians in public library settings, a busy library is much more likely to mean a busy librarian. In my experience and from conversations with public library colleagues, reference librarians in public libraries spend significant percentages of their time on the reference desk, helping patrons with research questions, readers' advisory requests, and technology issues. If you are a new librarian working in reference in a public library, you may quickly notice patterns and changes in your workload. It is still a good idea to ask an experienced colleague what to expect during particular times of year. Will there be an increase in homework-related help questions at the beginning of a new school year? How popular is the summer reading program at your branch? In many cases, the answers to these questions will be "yes" and "extremely popular," respectively. Particularly with larger public libraries, the library is a go-to resource for many information and entertainment needs of community members. Knowing when or if there will be slower times can help you plan ahead for projects.

The technical service work in public libraries may look different than it does in the academic setting. In larger systems, there may be a completely separate division (i.e., not in the same library branch) that orders and processes materials. If you are starting a job with a technical services focus in a public library (acquisitions, cataloging, etc.), you will probably notice trends similar to those in academic libraries—increases in work that correspond with ordering cycles.

Librarians in Other Work Settings

Librarians are not found only in public and academic libraries—we're everywhere! If you are seeking employment or starting a new position in a different area of librarianship, it is critical to make connections with professionals in that field to gain an understanding of the amount and intensity of the workload. I interviewed a school media specialist and found that, as the only professional in her library, she is responsible for filling all roles. Not only does she help students with reference and readers' advisory and teach classes on information skills, she is also responsible for ordering and processing books, managing the budget, taking care of administrative tasks, and providing technology support. In a one-person library, understanding the patterns of your workload will be even more important than in other settings. This media specialist's workload increases at the beginning and end of the school year, and her teaching load spikes at the end of each quarter. While she has a running list of tasks to complete, she is always prepared to change her priorities during those times to accomplish everything that needs to be done. This is valuable information to know, especially if you are not comfortable with constantly reprioritizing needs or if you have trouble changing directions quickly.

Special librarians, that umbrella term which encompasses so many information professionals, do such varied work that the life cycle of each year is likely to be completely unique. If you are starting a new position in a special library, begin tracking your time as soon as possible to identify peaks in your workload early on. Again, talk to others in the field and investigate the library literature to gain some understanding of how the work flows.

ANTICIPATE YOUR WORK FLOW AND PLAN ACCORDINGLY

Once you identify cycles in your workload, sketch out the life cycle of your year in your specific position. To use a typical year in my current position as an example, the cycles generally look like this:

- August–October: My calendar is very full, primarily with planning for and teaching information literacy sessions. I also co-teach a two-credit class during the fall semester, so August and September are particularly busy.

- November–December: With a more flexible calendar, I have more time to spend on my nonteaching responsibilities, including collection development, assessment, and service work.

- January–March: My calendar is full again with teaching. I have also noticed a slight increase in library and university committee work during the early spring.

- April–June: This is conference season, and I see an increase in research and creative work.

- July: My calendar is usually wide open, but I have plenty to do. This is the month I spend planning for the upcoming school year and doing all of the things I've been putting off "until summer" for the last year.

I suspected my time would fall this way in my current position because I worked closely with my predecessor. She gave me a heads-up about what I was in for my first fall semester, so I was able to plan accordingly. To accommodate my heavy class load, I reduced my reference desk hours for the fall, scaled back my research and creative activities, and did my best to take on fewer additional projects. I communicated this increase in workload to colleagues outside my department so that they have realistic expectations of the time I could commit to projects and committee work during this time period.

Anticipating your workload over the course of a year can also help you predict and plan for ebbs and flows in your personal energy and productivity levels. The dozens of library instruction sessions that I teach in September and October leave me little energy for other tasks and projects, so I save the bulk of my recurring, non-teaching work for November and December. Having this plan in place helps me balance my workload and adjust my work flow so that it is a better match for my energy levels. When I have more energy, I am also naturally more productive when it comes to tasks that require focus and concentration, like preparing for conference presentations or writing book chapters. If I do take on an additional project, I reevaluate and reallocate my time. I don't want to overcommit and fail to deliver. Having a sense of my other obligations keeps me from making that mistake. It is important for librarians to have realistic ideas of what they can accomplish, not only with a given number of hours in the day but also according to personal energy levels. We all need downtime, and that must be factored into the work flow. It is unrealistic to believe that you can teach several classes a week and then throw yourself headlong into a research project when the classes slow down. Everyone needs time to recharge.

Before you enter a new area of librarianship, it is a good idea to get a sense of the rhythms of the work to make sure that the position matches with your energy and productivity patterns. If you draw the most energy from helping the public, a technical services job might not be for you. If you are not a morning person, consider this carefully before accepting a position that requires an 8 a.m. service desk shift. You may even want to negotiate more flexible hours.

When you are new on a job, your supervisor can probably give you some sense of what your responsibilities will be in a given time period. If, for instance, you're a reference librarian at a public library and your main responsibility is to staff a busy reference desk six hours a day, you probably won't have the time or energy to devote to a system-wide project or a professional association committee. In fact, when starting a new position, it may be a wise to refrain from volunteering for major projects or committees until you know how much time you will have available for those types of commitments.

Another obligation that most librarians face is writing an annual self-evaluation. I have never met a librarian who loves to write the annual self-evaluation or report of accomplishments, regardless of the form it takes. One way I have made this less burdensome is to approach my self-evaluation as a way to look back over the year and determine whether the patterns I notice in the annual review match those that I have already identified. Generally, they do, although some years I may have taken on more committee work or attended fewer conferences. I use these patterns to forecast the following year, which is fortunate, as my institution requires us to submit our goals for the upcoming year and our summaries of the prior year at the same time. I also find my "What I did today" document invaluable as I prepare both my annual review and my goals.

FINAL THOUGHTS

I hope this chapter has given you some important information about the life cycle of your year. Yours will be unique to your personal situation, but it is critical for you to develop a familiarity with this cycle in order to be as effective as possible. Knowing what a typical year is like at your institution, even if you aren't yet able to forecast for your specific position, can help you develop a basic work plan. Having such a plan in place will help you be more productive and can also help you manage stress. Don't underestimate the value of your colleagues, within and beyond your institution. Talking to fellow librarians can be not only educational—and even therapeutic—but also an essential tool in managing the expectations you have of yourself and your work. When you have a handle on what's coming up, you will be better able to deal with the unexpected, the tasks and projects you didn't plan for, because you can work them into your existing plan.

ASSESSING THE JOB

Greta Wood

Whether you are new on the job or have been in your position a while, it is always useful to take time to assess what you are doing and decide when to ask for help. This chapter looks particularly at the tendency to "do it all" and how that can actually hurt you and your institution. It also gives strategies for determining how to evaluate and prioritize your workload.

THE STOP, DROP, AND ROLL APPROACH

Quiz anyone who attended elementary school in America about fire safety and one of their replies will be "Stop, drop, and roll." This series of three little steps, followed literally, will help you extinguish the flames if you ever catch on fire. Followed metaphorically, however, those three little words become a powerful guide for job success, whether you are new to the position or new to the profession. Think of it as a three-step program for job health: it coaches you to stop taking on more duties than you have the capacity to perform, to drop what you are doing and evaluate it, and to make sure that what you are doing is rolling in sync with your institution's or department's vision and goals. Ideal candidates for this approach are those who have more tasks than time, aren't sure how to prioritize those tasks, or wonder if those are even the tasks they should be prioritizing. If all you seem to be doing on your new job is putting out fires, remember that lesson from elementary school and stop, drop, and roll!

STOP BEING A HERO

One of the most personally transformative things I've read recently was librarian Jessamyn West's January 12, 2010, blog post "On Heroism" (www.librarian .net/stax/3126/on-heroism/), in which she quoted the following paragraph from Alex Payne's "Don't Be A Hero" post on software programming (https://al3x .net/2010/01/09/dont-be-a-hero.html):

> Heroes are damaging to a team because they become a crutch. As soon as you have someone who's always willing to work at all hours, the motivation from the rest of the team to produce reliable, trouble-free software drops. **The hero is a human patch.** Sure, you might sit around talking about how reliability is a priority, but in the back of your mind you know that the hero will be there to fix what doesn't work.

I went on to read Payne's original post, in which he explained that there's nothing wrong with being an occasional hero when long hours are required to complete a project, but being a perpetual hero is unsustainable and unscalable—and it leads to shortchanging yourself, your coworkers, and your customers. These two posts made me recognize the hero trait in myself and understand the downside of a seeming positive, and helped me accept that saying no was not necessarily a bad thing.

Shortchanging Yourself

Beyond shortchanging yourself on sleep and prep time, constantly being the hero shortchanges you in terms of time spent learning and developing the job you were hired to do. During my first year or so as a reference/instruction/catalog librarian at a small, private liberal arts university, I was drowning in instruction. I was new and wanted to be accommodating, so I accepted last-minute requests for instruction, requests for instruction at satellite locations in the evenings and on weekends, and requests for instruction when I was not scheduled to work. If a professor made a request, I was going to make it happen because I wanted the library to look good and, as the only instruction librarian, if I didn't do it, who would? After I became delirious (or was that deranged?) with instructional overload, I said no to a professor for the first time, and *nothing bad happened.* We rescheduled the session for another time and everything was fine. The next time I said no to a professor due to a time conflict, another librarian offered to conduct the session, and *everything was fine.* Giddy with my newfound ability to say no, I started taking control of my schedule and either offered alternate dates for the overflow or worked it out with another librarian to conduct the sessions during the originally requested time. No longer simply dashing back and forth between reference desk shifts and instruction sessions, I now had time to devote to my cataloging duties as well. I also had time to reflect on what was happening at the reference desk and during instruction sessions, and I could consider how I might improve my performance.

So the next time you find you're running yourself ragged because you don't know who would do these things if you don't, stop and evaluate what you are doing. Are you really the only one who can do this? Perhaps you are if you work in a specialized area or your library has a very small staff, but that doesn't mean that you have to do it *now*. If you are the only one who can perform a task or provide a service, take control of your schedule and collaborate with the requestor on an alternate date. Point out that by rescheduling you will have the time to offer them the best possible service, resulting in the best possible experience for both of you. If you are not the only one who can perform a task or provide a service, be honest about that and be willing to ask for help from a colleague. That old saying about only getting one chance to make a first impression is worth keeping in mind, but remember that it's not just you who's making an impression but the library as a whole, so protect the library brand by ensuring that your stakeholders have positive experiences with prepared professionals, not poor experiences with harassed heroes. Learn to say no and give yourself the time to think about what you are doing on the job.

This also includes thinking about *not* doing the job, or what would happen if you weren't there, either in the short term—you're out sick for a day—or the long term— you get promoted, retire, or leave for a different position. As an instruction librarian, I want my students to develop a transferrable skill set that they can take with them and use to become lifelong learners, but what about all of us as librarians? Should our skill sets be tethered to us as discrete individuals, or are they something that we should be embedding into, or transferring to, our jobs? In addition to thinking about *who* would do your job if you weren't there, also devote some time to thinking about *how* they would do your job. Are there protocols in place for storing your lesson plans on a shared network drive in case you wake up sick and there's no time to cancel an instruction session? Can you remotely access your lesson plan or handout and send it to another librarian? Is there a hard copy accessible in the building? These protocols should promote a transfer of knowledge and service performance as seamlessly as possible so the library can still function as a whole, even if the individuals within it change. I have created LibGuides that outline the assignment and include database searches with sample keywords. Beyond giving the students a search strategy to refer to when they start their own research, this also allows a substitute librarian to take over a presentation with very little preparation, or a new instruction librarian to get his or her feet wet without having to create lesson plans from scratch.

This type of "engineering for obsolescence" or "engineering for transference" is similar to what Jason B. Jones talks about in his *ProfHacker* post "Good University Service Means Self-Replacement" (http://chronicle.com/blogs/profhacker/good-uni versity-service-means-self-replacement/27892). He advises "that it's a handy thing, should you ever get elected to anything, to think a little about who'll replace you when your term is done. Because you should leave. It's good for your brain, and it's good for the university. It's also good for the soul to know that you're not irreplace-able." It may seem a bit odd to start thinking about who will replace you when you're new on the job, but thinking about how the next person in line will fulfill your duties will help you to focus on improving the functions of your job irrespective of who is performing them. Now, before you accuse me of sounding like the Borg in *Star Trek*, let me state that I am certainly not trying to downplay or devalue individual contri-butions or expertise—we all enjoy those satisfying "Look what I did" moments and deserve any associated accolades. But use those skills to "leave it better than you found it," as my dad often says. It could be fifty years before you "leave it," but leave it you will, and there is a world of difference between the appreciative sentiment "We couldn't have done it without you" and the panic-stricken sentiment "We can't do it without you." The first is empowering; the latter, destructive.

Shortchanging Coworkers

Perhaps counterintuitively, being the hero can end up shortchanging your cowork-ers rather than saving them. This can manifest as a sense of apathy toward library events similar to the lack of motivation engendered by the human patch in Payne's description, a sort of inertia created by the knowledge that someone else will always volunteer to do the job, or it can manifest as a sense of disconnect from the library and its purpose, a sort of disengagement created by feelings of resentment or pow-erlessness. Coworkers may feel their help is not welcome or that their suggestions won't make a difference anyway if someone else always monopolizes the opportuni-ties to contribute.

If you find that you're the one being the hero, it may be time to learn how to say no and stop shutting others out of the process. This may not sound like the usual sort of job advice, but by saying no you are creating an opportunity for someone else as well as some extra time for yourself. This may be an opportunity born out of the silence created when you don't volunteer, a silence that will hopefully be filled by someone else overcoming their inertia and volunteering, or it may be an opportunity born out of your willingness to recommend someone else for a project, a willingness that will hopefully show your coworkers that you value their expertise and are willing to share the spotlight. It is said that the ability to delegate is the sign of a good leader, so make it about what "we accomplished" and not about what "I did." Sometimes you'll contribute less, sometimes more, and it's that ebb and flow which makes for a sustainable work pace. If you are always the hero, you will simply burn out and, along the way, begin to resent your coworkers for not contributing as much as you. This affects morale and the cohesiveness of your team and ultimately leads to a dysfunctional staff. Who knew that something so lauded in our society as heroism could produce such disastrous results!

If someone else has become the accepted yes-person at your institution, consider beating them to the volunteer draw or explicitly speaking up and saying something like, "I'm interested in learning more about that. Could I work with you on that project?" Since you are new on the job, always be mindful of how these efforts are received and start small and work slowly. Things do not always happen quickly in academia or in government agencies and this, if you're like me and came to librarianship from the corporate world, can take some getting used to.

Shortchanging Customers

Many of us have experienced the "baby duck" syndrome with patrons: you help patrons, solve a technical problem, or teach an instruction session, and all of a sudden you become "their" librarian. They imprint on you and believe no one else can help them. While this is flattering, do not let their preference for you go to your head, because having a hero on staff does not create a better user experience. Sure, it might solve an immediate issue, but it does not create an ongoing sustainable system of service. In general—barring in-depth subject-specific consultations, special collections requests, and the like—you should not have patrons scheduling their visits according to when a certain staff member is on duty or have librarians telling patrons that they'll have to wait for a specific librarian to help them. If you do, your library has a problem.

If you are the only one who knows a certain trick in the circulation system, or that a certain program works best in a certain browser and crashes in another, or that a certain resource is the best solution for a class assignment, and you don't share this knowledge with your fellow librarians except when you swoop in to save the day for the patron, what happens when you are not there? Patrons should have an expectation of service continuity and quality irrespective of staff scheduling, and if that expectation is not met, what happens to the patron's opinion of the library and the rest of its employees? Having a hero on staff might build a sense of dependence in patrons upon a certain librarian, but it doesn't build a sense of trust in the library and its systems as a whole.

"But if the patron was helped, what does it matter?" you may wonder. It matters a great deal for many reasons, including morale and the healthy functioning of the library. It especially matters when it's time for budget decisions. If positive opinion is linked to an individual and not to the library in general, how does the library lobby for a budget increase? How does it fight against budget cuts? How does it convince the public to vote for a tax increase that would support the entire library system when it's really only the one librarian that they care about? If public, student, faculty, or administrative estimation of the library's worth is based on the performance of one individual, what happens to the perceived value of the library when that person leaves?

I have mentioned the library brand once already in this chapter—understandably since I worked in advertising in my prelibrarian life—and it bears repeating a second time: brand loyalty to the library lasts long into the future, but a cult of personality lasts only as long as that person's tenure. So take yourself out of the picture and refocus your efforts on making the library the star.

DROP WHAT YOU ARE DOING AND EVALUATE

A January 11, 2011, ResourceShelf's *ResourceBlog* article presented a portion of a draft copy of the Center for Technology in Government at the University of Albany's brief "Designing Social Media Policy for Government," which outlined three types of social media use by government employees: agency use, professional use, and personal use (http://web.resourceshelf.com/go/resourceblog/63202). I read this article shortly after being invited to contribute to this book, and it provided a perfect scaffold for assessing the job.

If you find you are developing a sort of occupational attention deficit disorder and don't know or can't decide what to do next, drop everything for a moment and evaluate where each of your current tasks fits: agency use, professional use, or personal use. You can also look at each task and evaluate whether you are doing it for your institution, your profession, or yourself. Either way, it boils down to (1) job duties; (2) professional development; and (3) personal interest. So take a little time and tally up the tick marks, see how your efforts are spread across the board, and determine if you need to reallocate some of the time and energy you are spending on each category.

Some job descriptions weight each major area of responsibility with actual percentages of time. This can be a big help in prioritizing your duties, but if yours does not, you can still get a good idea of what duties should occupy a majority of your time by reviewing your job description on your own or with your supervisor. Then keep a time sheet for a few weeks and cross-examine what your job description says with what your actual time spent reveals. To take this exercise a step further, compare your findings with the job descriptions for job titles similar to yours on library job sites such as INALJ (I Need a Library Job eResource Center), ALA JobLIST, or the *Chronicle of Higher Education*'s jobs database. This will help you evaluate how well your job title and description compare to accepted standards for that position in the profession, as well as give you a good idea of how competitive a candidate you might be to potential search committees if you ever apply to a different library.

Once you have a clear(er) grasp of how your job performance is aligning with your job description, you can use that data to figure the time/reward equation when deciding whether to take on additional duties. If you are light on institutional service, it might be good to accept an invitation to sit on or chair a committee. If you are light on professional development, perhaps it's time to take a continuing education course. If you are solid on both institutional and professional activities, perhaps you can devote some time to developing a personal interest. By personal interest I don't mean opera lessons—unless you are the liaison to the music or theater department—but something that intrigues you professionally that isn't part of your normal sphere of influence on the job. You may be a cataloger with an interest in genealogy, so you might collaborate with local history organizations or offer workshops on using online databases for genealogical research. Or like me, you might find yourself doing something totally unexpected that fulfills institutional, professional, and personal goals.

It happened like this. I was whirring along in my aforementioned reference/instruction/catalog librarian position when suddenly we no longer had an access services manager, which meant, at our academic library of eight total staff members, that we had no access services department. Until the position was filled and the new person trained, our director handled the billing and ordering of office supplies, our circulation supervisor helped out with Friends of the Library duties, and I found myself processing interlibrary loan requests. I had some previous interlibrary loan experience so the transition wasn't too bumpy, but our volume didn't justify an automated system like ILLiad, so I was looking at a serious time commitment in manually processing all article lending and all article and book borrowing requests in OCLC Resource Sharing (we had one student assistant who processed the book lending requests).

Declining wasn't an option since I was the only one who could take over these duties without a big interruption in service or in my daily job performance. But did the time commitment provide any value or reward to my main functions of reference, instruction, and cataloging? Oddly, the answer is yes, and then some. These new duties provided a service to my institution, but they also provided me with concrete takeaways that were useful in my day-to-day job function, as described later. In addition, they allowed me to satisfy a personal research quirk. Through processing the requests and evaluating how patrons filled out the forms, I started to get a clearer picture of how my constituents found materials and what they understood in regard to those materials via what citation elements were left out and/or entered incorrectly. This had a direct impact on the content of my instruction, as I focused more on how to determine if our library had access to a certain resource and how to identify what that resource was based on its citation components. I also became more familiar with what students and faculty requested that our library resources did not cover, which in turn strengthened my collection development efforts. Plus, processing these requests satisfied my puzzle-loving brain—I hated to see a request go unfilled—and it gave me a great sense of accomplishment to track down difficult-to-locate resources or find free access to articles in open-access journal archives.

So, in addition to making the library and university look good by providing uninterrupted and efficient service, I was able to enhance my professional value by learning more about the research habits of my patrons, all while satisfying my inner detective. Not a bad return on the time/reward equation.

ROLL WITH YOUR COMMANDER'S INTENT

In her *ACRLog* guest post "Ready, Set, Teach: You in the Classroom" (http://acrlog .org/2010/09/08/ready-set-teach-you-in-the-classroom/), Sarah Faye Cohen refers to the military concept of commander's intent (CI), which she read about in *Made to Stick: Why Some Ideas Survive and Others Die* by Chip and Dan Heath (Random House, 2007). She quotes the following from page 26 of their book: "CI is a crisp, plain-talk statement that appears at the top of every order, specifying the plan's goal, the desired end-state of an operation . . . the CI never specifies so much detail that it risks being rendered obsolete by unpredictable events." She then reinterprets the concept of commander's intent as knowing your core intent, which resonated with me, as it gave me a name to put to my tendency to ask goal-seeking questions in various aspects of my job. From library marketing efforts to instructional content selection to cataloging projects, when I asked, "What is our/my goal with this?" or "What do we/I hope to accomplish with this?" or "What is the purpose of this?" I was trying to define my core intent. This, in turn, defined the task's scope, parameters, and basis for evaluation.

In one of the first meetings of a new committee convened at a previous work-place, I was thrilled when a faculty member queried the chair, "What are we charged with?" Without an answer to this question, with no clear expectations or scope for guiding themselves and their efforts, the time/reward equation for members serving on that committee would just implode and collapse into a black hole of aimless meetings. If you don't know what your core intent is, ask, but make it an informed question. There are a number of resources you can consult based on the situation to help you determine what your core intent should be, such as your institutional, library, or departmental mission statements, your job description and criteria for annual review, and your supervisor's goals.

For example, many library mission statements incorporate access to information as one of their primary goals. Get out that job evaluation sheet you created earlier in this chapter to see if activities listed on it support access to information in some way. I would bet that, regardless of your job title, you perform some function that fulfills your library's core intent of supporting access to information. It might be as a webmaster who works on accessibility issues, a cataloger who cleans up MARC records, or an e-resources manager who negotiates contracts with vendors. However, as you continue to tie each of the items on your evaluation check sheet to a component of your departmental or institutional mission statement, eventually you will come across one or more items that just don't fit anywhere or give you any payoff in the time/reward equation. These may be candidates for demotion on or removal from your priority list, in consultation with your supervisor. Aligning your work efforts with your institutional, departmental, and supervisory expectations will ensure that your core intent supports, and is supported by, your commander's intent.

FINAL THOUGHTS

So maybe you did learn everything you need to know in kindergarten. If the mantra "Stop, drop, and roll" can save you when you literally are on fire, it can probably do the same when you just feel like everything is going up in flames. Remember to stop being a hero and trying to do it all, drop everything for a moment and take

What to Do when You Are Engulfed in Flames

- Stop trying to do it all.
- Drop everything, take a deep breath, and prioritize.
- Roll with the goal that is most important.

time to critically evaluate and assess your job, and then make sure that your workload choices moving forward are rolling in harmony with your commander's or your core intent. This can help get you on track when you are new on the job, but it can also help keep you on track as you progress in your career. As Ranganathan's fifth law of library science states, "The library is a growing organism," and missions, needs, and goals will change over time. Therefore, successful evaluation and assessment must involve continual reevaluation and reassessment, so let's add one more word to our mantra to keep everything running smoothly: Stop, drop, roll, repeat.

DEVELOPING A PLAN B

Beth Martin

In today's economic climate, it pays for librarians who are job hunting to be able to think outside the box. Are there employment possibilities outside of libraries for librarians? How do you present yourself to potential employers to capitalize on skills you learned in library school? This chapter addresses developing a Plan B and includes creative ways to present yourself in person and on your résumé to make the most of the skills you learned in library school.

IN THE BEGINNING

I decided to become a librarian while working evenings in the library of a small liberal arts college to help finance my MA degree. In the library I discovered a perfect mix of people, technology, and information. I realized that is where I wanted to have a career. I enrolled in a Library and Information Studies program, graduated, and began the job search. That is when the necessity of a Plan B first came to the forefront.

I applied for everything—any professional position in a library—and I was getting nowhere. I began to worry that I had spent two years on a library and information science (LIS) degree and would never find a job in my area. It was discouraging. During this time a friend called and asked me if I knew anyone who would be interested in a position with her company. As she described the position, I thought, "I can do that . . . what about me?" I began to analyze the skills I had gained through my library science education and realized those skills transcended libraries and would be useful to many employers. With so many people looking for ways to navigate the information landscape, I saw opportunities for people like me who could help them. That is how I ended up with a wonderful position as a communication specialist for information security at a large financial institution. This chapter explains how I thought outside the library and formulated my personal Plan B. It also addresses how you can think of yourself in different ways and learn to express those thoughts to potential employers.

The first obstacle I encountered in applying for positions outside libraries was the perception of what it means to have a degree in library and information science, or overcoming the stereotypes of what a "librarian" does or is. Regardless of how much we may love the term, and I do love being a librarian, it does not translate to all fields. You must be prepared to define yourself in new ways and to convey that definition to those outside the field. This is made easier by the fact you are still doing what you want to do—putting people in touch with information. *Information professional* is a great way to describe your skills when you are looking for positions outside of libraries. *Research analyst* and *competitive intelligence* are also good job search terms as well as new ways to describe your skills. Once you have innovative ways to describe yourself, use these terms to search for new positions. This is not the time to be self-effacing and limit yourself by feeling inadequate because you are "only" a librarian. This is the time to use all of your assets creatively.

I have found that developing an elevator speech is a good way to dispel the view potential employers may have of your skills as a librarian. An elevator speech is a concise description of your abilities—a speech you can give to a potential employer in the time it takes to ride an elevator a few floors. The process of preparing an elevator speech forces you to consider everything you bring to a new working environment and prepares you to answer questions from potential employers.

The Pepperdine Business School offers this advice on elevator speeches: know your audience; know yourself; outline your talk; finalize your speech (http://bschool.pe perdine.edu/career/content/elevatorspeech.pdf). Knowing yourself means that you consider what you have to offer as an information professional. Begin outlining your

---

Describing Yourself in New Ways

QUESTION: What can you, as a librarian, bring to our organization?

ANSWER: My ability to quickly locate relevant information and communicate it in a variety of mediums and for a variety of audiences. My skills will help you disseminate the appropriate information to your constituents.

talk by writing down key points and then develop ideas from these key points. Be sure to finalize your speech with practice. It is a good idea to keep the speech under thirty seconds, so practice with a friend or in front of a mirror. The elevator speech is useful in interviews because it concisely describes what you, as an information professional, have to offer. It is important to know your audience because you do not want to be too general. In other words, tailor your speech to meet the needs of the organization. This should be easy because you already have a wide range of experiences with audience needs since information professionals must know their audience when collecting materials, marketing services, and teaching classes. You may have even created pathfinders or taught information literacy courses designed for biology majors or ESL students. All of these skills prepare you to meet the needs of a variety of constituents.

Sample Elevator Speech

Here is the elevator speech that I used when applying for an information security position. I used it to open the interview and then built on the topics throughout the process.

Your organization maintains information security for all the customers. I understand the many ways information is disseminated to various groups and how it can be used in ways that were never intended. My education gives me the ability to understand customer information needs and the ability to research issues that may threaten the information security of your customers. I am well equipped to work with your team to meet these threats head-on by keeping the security specialists up to date on current issues and by creating presentations that clearly and concisely explain the threats. My expertise will allow your team to make quick, informed decisions that will protect your customers and your organization.

RÉSUMÉ AND COVER LETTER

It may seem obvious, but don't forget to reexamine your résumé and cover letter with your new definitions about the profession. The cover letter is a vital component of any job search and allows you to expand on the elevator speech. The letter should address your skills as an information professional, not as "just" a librarian. Never use a generic cover letter; craft one that fits the position for which you are applying and that explains how your degree enhances your skills. Use your elevator speech as a guide to writing your letter as you explain how your degree is useful in the position and how it will enhance the services you deliver.

In addition to a good cover letter, a skills résumé is an excellent way to highlight the experience you bring to a new position. Part of the challenge is communicating your experience and how your LIS degree enhances your skills. A skills résumé focuses on your value to a potential employer in ways that go beyond a chronological list of jobs. Begin a skills résumé with a list of attributes that you will offer to a new employer such as project management, customer service, technology knowledge, and research skills. Highlight any projects you have done that reflect these particular skills. This type of résumé is also useful for career changers who have a lot of experience in a different area, but experience that others may perceive as irrelevant. Skills résumés highlight the similarities between your roles in other positions—as a student and as a professional—that translate to a variety of roles.

WHAT I DID OUTSIDE THE LIBRARY

The best way to relate my nontraditional position with the skills I gained in library school is to describe my duties in relation to the student learning outcomes in my graduate program. The student learning outcomes were used for the final student evaluation when graduating from my LIS program. At the time of my graduation there were five overarching student learning outcomes (http://lis.uncg.edu/):

1. The student demonstrates an understanding of the social, legal, and ethical foundations of library and information science.
2. The student is able to evaluate and apply current research and thought in the field of management.
3. The student demonstrates the ability to design effective solutions to meet the information needs of patrons.
4. The student demonstrates an understanding of collection development principles appropriate to the mission of the parent organization.
5. The student understands and applies information technology for the improvement of library services.

These outcomes are addressed in a variety of courses and cover much of the profession; however, I believe they are also useful in describing how my skills were used outside of a traditional information agency.

Goal 1

The student demonstrates an understanding of the social, legal, and ethical foundations of library and information science. Information ethics is a key component of an LIS program. As information professionals we are asked to consider various forms of information and how much information should be "free" or "open" to our constituents. There are legal aspects, challenges even, to maintaining a collection or harvesting information. In terms of technology, with so much open access, it is up to us to understand the legal ramifications of information use. We often deal with this in terms of copyright or collection management, but the theories of information access traverse a wide landscape and should be considered when composing your Plan B. In other words, don't get locked into thinking of your library experiences too narrowly. Try to see them in a broader context.

In my work as a communication specialist for corporate information security for a large financial organization, I was often called upon to work with security information that could be accessed only by specific colleagues. While it is easy to believe that financial information should be private, it is important to articulate why. I needed to understand the culture of the company and the ramifications to our customers. In what way does the information we provide help our customers, and how should it be disseminated? What are the ethics and corporate responsibility about collecting customer information, and with whom should we share this information? Customers need to be aware of security risks; however, we must consider ways to share this information that doesn't cause a public risk. As information professionals we are well equipped to discuss these questions from all sides to help reach a solution that is good for all constituents.

Goal 2

The student is able to evaluate and apply current research and thought in the field of management. Management courses not only teach you how to become a manager but also help you understand managers' needs. My ability to quickly find and understand information was useful for my managers when they were preparing reports or making security decisions. This type of skill would be an asset in jobs inside and outside libraries. In addition, I built on my management coursework by expanding my interaction with colleagues at all levels of the organization. I was able to take my knowledge of management and apply it to security organizations in a way that helped shape decisions.

I found that one of the best items for management is the executive summary, which is a concise, synthesized account of what the larger presentation discusses. The ability to create this summary was an essential part of my management class and carried over to all of my subsequent positions. Information professionals are trained to filter out extraneous information and find that which is most relevant, which means they are already trained to write effective executive summaries.

Goal 3

The student demonstrates the ability to design effective solutions to meet the information needs of patrons. We do this when we design tutorials on information literacy or how to navigate a catalog. We do this when we create pathfinders or websites so our constituents can find information. We do this when we teach information tailored to the appropriate audience. These are transferable skills and can help constitute a plan for opportunities outside of libraries.

Sharing information in my new setting was done primarily through Microsoft PowerPoint presentations, otherwise known as a "deck." Part of my job was to highlight the relevant information in PowerPoint. The information was in small font, and there were numerous columns. I found it confusing, and it was difficult for people to make decisions based on these PowerPoint slides. I set about changing this and began to use images, maps, graphs, and tables in ways that better displayed information and were more easily understood. I knew that corporate communication styles need to be used to maximum effectiveness, and my experience as an information professional helped make this possible.

Goal 4

The student demonstrates an understanding of collection development principles appropriate to the mission of the parent organization. I performed regular environmental scans on various information security sites. In addition, I returned to these sites based upon the information needs of the community to create presentations or reports. I collected stories and statistics for my department, which were also useful for my colleagues as they prepared security reports, analyses, and new technologies. I also collected presentations, being careful about the ones that were protected. They were not all for everyone to see or use—another important part of collection management.

The company often had "911" or "drive by" emergencies. Essentially, a manager would run to my desk and state that we needed some information in a PowerPoint format within the next two hours. I was able to call upon my reserve of information, graphics, and tables to create the needed information in time for the emergency meeting. This often occurred when we experienced a security issue that needed to be addressed immediately. My collection included past presentations, websites, articles, and graphics. I also kept a collection of websites with up-to-the-minute data on information security threats around the world that I could use for my presentations. The ability to manage data is key in any fast-paced environment where decisions must be made in minutes. This is something that all librarians are trained to do.

Goal 5

The student understands and applies information technology for the improvement of library services. Information and communication requests came to me primarily via e-mail or word of mouth. There was no tracking system, no way to manage requests, and no way for clients to follow the progress of their requests. I worked with a colleague to design a system that allowed clients to make and track requests through the information life cycle. Clients could log in to the system to see projected completion dates, ask questions, and make changes to the requests. The organizational skills I learned in library school served me well.

The organization also rolled out a new social media site just for employees' internal use. Through the site, I created a window into my collection of websites, presentations, and links to helpful books. The corporation also allowed blogging on topics that could be useful for sharing information. I also used this site to discuss tips on creating informative presentations and the best ways to disseminate information within the organization.

WAYS TO CREATE A PLAN B

One of the best things you can do to prepare for Plan B is to start before you ever graduate from library school. Begin by visiting your career center to find help in crafting example résumés. These examples can help you later when you update your résumé for new positions and career possibilities. In addition, the career center can help you define your skills and advise you on how to approach prospective employers outside the library field. Career centers know employers in your area and how you can best fit their needs.

Vet your résumés with nonlibrary professionals when looking for positions outside traditional information agencies. Those outside the profession can help identify library-specific jargon that may not be obvious to those in the profession. These reviewers can also identify areas that may be of more use to potential employers and can suggest ways to market your skills to this new audience.

In addition, stay in touch with other LIS alumni after graduation. They can be valuable resources in your job search. Often they are the first to know about new opportunities and can keep you updated. Friends and former colleagues outside of the profession can also suggest opportunities. A friend and former colleague suggested that I apply for a job at her company because she could speak to my interoffice abilities. She also knew what I had done in graduate school and that my new skills, combined with my previous work experience, would bring an additional dimension to the position.

Whether still in library school or out in the working world, it is always a good idea to make new contacts through professional organizations such as your local library association. Smaller regional or state organizations are less costly to join and allow you to network with others in your area. Join or renew all the associations you can at the student rate because it is much more expensive upon graduation. Use social media to keep up with trends, jobs, and discussions. Groups often sponsor free discussions on topics relevant to libraries and may compile a list of job opportunities in a variety of information agencies. Search the social media sites for terms related to information professions to find groups that may help you keep up your skills. Facebook has groups to keep you in touch with professional organizations and those in the field.

Friending your alumni organization on Facebook is a great way to keep up with free talks and continuing education. Industries that focus on information agencies often offer free webinars about their products. This is an excellent way to stay on top of industry trends. Volunteer at places you would like to work. This leads to new contacts and puts you in a better position when a job becomes available.

The American Library Association offers electronic discussion lists in many areas of interest. For example, there is an information literacy list where professionals post items of interest as well as job openings. Local organizations may support "unconferences" that cater to those in the information industry. These are usually free and allow the audience to choose the topics. You can attend sessions or lead a session in your area. Leading a session gives you the opportunity to meet people who can help you add to your skills as well as suggest job opportunities. Leading a session also gives you a platform for showcasing your teaching abilities and other skills. These events help highlight your versatility and that of the profession as a whole.

Another way to refine your Plan B is to join Friends of the Library groups at various institutions. In academic libraries, a friends group is a great way to stay current with library website design, database changes, and other information tools. Public libraries often have friends groups that you can participate in and even help plan events. This allows you to further the cause of your local libraries as well as maintain your skills.

After you graduate, stay in touch with professors who helped you in graduate school, especially those who focused on your interest areas and took the time to write letters of recommendation. Your professors have invested in you and want to see you succeed. They are often eager to help you find a position. I can personally attest to this, as my professors have helped me throughout my career and continue to encourage me in my new position.

HOW I WENT BACK TO A LIBRARY

I really enjoyed my work outside of libraries, but my ultimate goal was to return to an academic library, and so I stayed in touch with the LIS world. I maintained my membership in associations such as the North Carolina Library Association and the American Library Association. I maintained contacts with colleagues from graduate school as well as those in other types of libraries. I continued to read about the field and stay abreast of changes in the profession. I used RSS feeds to gather information about jobs. I also followed the *Chronicle of Higher Education* job posts (http://chroniclevitae.com/job_search/new) and other library sites for my region. When a job appeared that caught my interest, I contacted friends to ask if they knew anyone at the library. Colleagues and former classmates can often help you get your foot in the door for that crucial first meeting with a potential employer. Employing a reverse version of Plan B, I incorporated my experience as a corporate information professional into my résumé for library positions. My experiences highlighted my versatility as an employee and demonstrated what I could bring to any situation. This versatility has been the key to my employment both inside and outside of libraries. The ability to accept change and be a change agent is critical for today's information professional and is something to cultivate as you move through your career.

I continued to apply for library positions throughout my tenure in the corporate world. It eventually paid off because an employer had kept my information on file to review again as new positions came open. Librarians at the university spoke with their colleagues about me, and I was invited to an interview. My colleagues and former classmates helped me get through that first door; my experience in the corporate world opened the door even wider. I was offered the perfect position in an academic library as an instructional technology librarian, teaching information literacy and exploring new technologies for the library.

These experiences later helped me move into a position as a program coordinator for an LIS program, teaching, advising, and collaborating with people entering library school. Because of my previous work experience, I am able to help students recognize the value of past work experiences that they bring to the field. Many are changing careers and/or come from all types of undergraduate experiences, and I help them express their experiences in the language of the profession. I am excited to see people bring new ideas to the profession and then share what they learn in the program with new audiences. These students are opening more doors into areas outside of libraries and are displaying our skills to a broader public. It is an exciting time to explore your Plan B.

Because I know the value of creating a Plan B when a library job isn't available, and the value of using my experiences once I return to the field of librarianship, I am uniquely qualified to help others craft their Plan Bs.

A CONTINUING JOURNEY

I believe my experience as an information professional outside of a traditional library enhanced my positions inside libraries. I was asked to join administrative committees such as the Quality Enhancement Plan Committee, which performs long-term strategic planning. My Plan B helped me reach Plan A in a short time and enhanced my skills as a librarian. As I transitioned into a role in an LIS program, I realized how all of my experiences as a librarian, teacher, and information professional prepared me for tasks I had not originally envisioned. It has and continues to be a wonderful journey.

It will serve you well to maintain contacts in both traditional and nontraditional information agencies. Be sure to keep up with changes in the field, as this will prepare you for future challenges. People may tell you to think outside the box, but I suggest you don't get in the box in the first place. Open yourself to a variety of experiences and they will all shape the way you work as an information professional—your Plan B may be just what you were looking for all along.

HOW NOT TO BE ONE OF THE PENGUINS

Phil Blank

While traditional work in libraries is a good fit for most people who have pursued a library studies degree, some librarians actually function better outside of libraries. One path to finding a niche for yourself outside of a library is to identify something innovative that you want to pursue. In my case, I became interested in virtual reference when it was new, and I was able to follow that interest to a position overseeing a statewide virtual reference program. This chapter looks at the best and worst of being a penguin and might help you decide where you fit.

IN PRAISE OF PENGUINS

First, I must recognize that penguins, or so-called "conventional" librarians, are amazing people and an admirable thing to want to be. As anyone knows who has watched the YouTube video "March of the Librarians" (www.youtube.com/watch?v=Td9221 0NoDQ), librarians can appear to be a homogenous group who all act and work the same. Such lack of individuality can seem unappealing, but what the video doesn't convey is that penguins accomplish much in the field.

I came into librarianship because I liked what librarians did. I also liked what they didn't do. They didn't handle a lot of money, they didn't seem overly stressed, and they didn't seem to suffer the many small indignities that overcome workers in many other professions. But I didn't understand how hard some librarians worked until I met and worked alongside some penguins. They taught me much, especially a respect for the profession of librarianship.

I remember R. S., a librarian with whom I worked at a Brooklyn Public Library branch. Because after-school programs were being cut across the city due to severe budget constraints, the library quickly became a place for students to gather after school. Most of the students were great, but a few were so disruptive that the library's longtime patrons moved to the margins or stopped coming in at all. The effect of losing our core constituents and of dealing with an array of problems was a worsening morale among librarians and a steady series of compromises in programming and service. But R. S. never wavered. He insisted on providing the best services he could no matter how difficult. That's a penguin—willing to continue marching along in the cold. I found that admirable.

My next lesson came in the academic setting. S. C. was a powerhouse, cranking out more webpages than the rest of the department combined. In fact, he was like his own department, making his own goals and plowing through them mercilessly. The years didn't wear him down. He thrived on the profession and added much to it. He's still out there, still doing amazing things—another testament to penguinism.

Of course, these days, the unconventional is celebrated everywhere. It is touted as a way to freedom or an expression of the individuality at the heart of our culture. Unfortunately, this culture still embraces the old stereotype of librarians as straight-laced, bun-wearing squares, toiling away among dusty books. Although I was always impressed by the unconventional life of librarians, I may have subconsciously accepted some of these cultural assumptions about their working lives. If I came into librarianship for its unconventional people, I certainly was equally surprised and enriched by the "conventional" ones—those who did their jobs well, those who thrived on the organizational skills at the heart of the work.

ADVENTURES IN PENGUINSHIP

My fascination with librarians began when I was a child. My hometown was a dreadfully conservative suburb north of Philadelphia. The librarians were different from the other adults around me. They were buying books and records outside the mainstream. As a teenager I found records by the Fugs, Sonny Terry, and Brownie Mc-Ghee (a record that began a lifelong fascination with instrumental and vernacular music). Our library had three books on the early twentieth-century Austrian painter

Egon Schiele years before he became a popular sensation. Who were these librarians who added such unique items to the collection? How did they know about all of these treasures? That library taught me more about the culture of the world than my school or family, simply by putting it out there and letting me loose.

Our library was also one of those staffed by "unconventional" people. At my age, this meant people who were different from the other adults I knew. I remember the tone of the reference librarian as she described how the biography section worked. What lingered was that here was a professional person who talked to me as an equal. This was a different relationship from those I had with teachers or other adults. Also, she valued books enough to work with them all day, which automatically made her something of a freak in my world. As I got older, I became aware of the larger history of unconventional people in libraries, everything from gender and sexual orientations to a much more diverse group of people whose values were radically different from those of mainstream America. There were also many conventional librarians, including one who would never check out a book from the library because "they're filthy!!!"

In college I worked in the university art library, where I saw a sector of librarianship I call "academic skid row." By this I mean those who come to the profession from academia, mostly in flight from the battleground of the doctorate. This is a part of the profession that is seldom talked about, perhaps because it maintains the assumption that librarians are "less than teachers." This is not true. Some of these folks may be a little shell-shocked by their time as students, but others were insightful people who were liberated by leaving academia. They weren't called to the library profession originally, but they were great colleagues and excellent librarians—and they were definitely not penguins. It was from these librarians that I got a further view of independent thinkers.

This was the early 1990s and the art world was lost in a haze of ego and postmodernism. When I graduated from college, a professor called me into his office and asked if I had considered being an art history graduate student. Part of me wanted that, but a larger part craved a life of practical service. I wanted a job where I knew I'd be helpful, and I had seen that in the library. I blurted out, "I'm going to be a librarian."

The next year I enrolled in library science graduate school. The reference classes were excellent, and other classes less so. We referred to them as library "scientology" classes because of the lack of scientific rigor. I couldn't muster the effort to try very hard in these classes. Instead I spent hours in the library, got involved in the community's arts and music culture, and enjoyed my last years of life as a student. My real education came on the reference desk where I worked as a graduate student, a job that gave me a feel for both the needs of patrons and how administrations worked. My image of the stress-free librarian with a lot of autonomy took a hit, as I saw bosses fret over budgets and knock heads with other departments.

PUBLIC PENGUINS

My first job as a professional librarian was in one of the Brooklyn Public Library's branches. This was my introduction to intense penguinism. My boss ran a tight ship when it came to punctuality, paperwork, and procedure. Because I only had a short time for lunch, and it seemed my boss was timing me to the second, I was always wolfing down lunches and watching the clock. Sometimes I simply had to run errands, and when I did I felt panicked. I didn't get off work until five and the bank closed at five—always a source of stress!

This was penguinism at its worst, or librarianship by the numbers. At least one day of the week I double-checked other people's time cards. Every task seemed to involve paperwork that took twice as long as the task itself. When it finally seemed beyond absurd, I tried to find ways to amuse myself while getting the task done. This approach took me only so far, and I continued to chafe under the regimentation.

Still, I probably could have endured it if we were also providing quality service. I remember the first day on the job. I was welcomed, the rules were explained, and I was directed to my desk. Of course, there was nothing to do, so after sharpening my pencils and making sure my pens worked, I walked out to the juvenile area, pulled a book off the shelf, and started to read. I was trying out this library to see how it felt to be in it. Within seconds, some children came around and I began to read the book aloud to them. My boss was not pleased. He explained that unless I was scheduled to be on the reference desk, I was to be in my office.

So I was forced into my office, where I spent many hours after my work was finished literally trapped in the office, of service to no one but fulfilling my obligation to stay in the building a certain number of hours. This is one of the ways that I believe librarians, or anyone, can be made into penguins. While this could work for some people, I knew it couldn't work for me. I started to plan for an unconventional working situation that would allow me more autonomy. I recognized that I wanted this, but I just wasn't sure how to make it happen. I suspect that I was like many people who realize they need a change. The idea percolates for a long time before it becomes fully formed.

Meanwhile, I began to look for ways to bring some change and create some independence for myself where I was. The branch where I worked had discipline issues with the after-school crowd. After a serious incident involving two girls with scissors fighting with each other, I decided to start a debate club or, as I called it, "Jimmy" Springer. Jimmy Springer was to resemble the TV show *Jerry Springer* but much more managed. We would pick a topic of debate and have two contestants argue their sides. They were given time to find material in the library, which would help them score points, and the audience was repeatedly called upon to judge whether their arguments were fair. In no time, Jimmy Springer became extremely popular. However, my boss was not as enthusiastic, noting that this sort of programming would not be offered in a wealthier community and also pointing out that it reeked of danger. In the end, nothing bad ever happened, and it did add structure and some educational value to the library. In hindsight, I think I was searching for creative ways to find my place in a library. My goal was to do something that would enable the library to function as usual for those who wanted that and basically provide a distraction for others who were simply looking for something to do. It was empowering to be able to think about the problem and to experiment with solutions.

I think many people reach the point in their career where they realize they are either content with the work environment they are in or they realize it isn't right for them and they have to get out. Once you make the decision that a traditional library setting isn't right, this is a good time to cast around for innovations to be made in the library or in the field that have a greater appeal. Once you identify something that excites you, educate yourself further and put out gentle feelers in the library community about the possibility of employment doing that work.

HOW I LEFT THE FLOCK

During my time in Brooklyn, I rediscovered my interest in art and wanted more time to pursue my own art. However, I didn't want to leave my steady paycheck and benefits. I kept looking for a solution that would work better for me. I read a lot of job announcements and finally found what I was looking for in an academic library job in North Carolina working thirty-five hours a week. Technically this was a part-time job, but thirty-five was the magic number that allowed me to still receive benefits. In my spare time I worked on my paintings and tried to make enough money to compensate for the lost time. It was the best of both worlds and was made possible only by a temporary need of the college's reference department. They had something else that I found incredibly liberating—flex time.

Flex time meant that my schedule was fluid as long I met my hourly requirements and showed up at the reference desk when I was scheduled to be there. Along with this came a huge leap in human dignity. My boss allowed me to stretch flex time to its limits once I proved that I was able to do my work competently and on time. I met others who were working in unconventional ways and at unconventional hours. In fact, the technical staff had elevated flex time into a high art form. It was common for them to work overnight and go home when the rest of the staff showed up at 8:00 in the morning. Sometimes they worked marathon shifts and then took extra days off. Yet they still accomplished their jobs and did so well. They seemed even more unusual in their private lives, practicing martial arts on the university lawn, dressing eccentrically, but also pursuing their own creative goals behind the security of their positions.

WORKING AN UNCONVENTIONAL SCHEDULE

While in the academic library, I was appointed to be in charge of implementing the library's virtual reference software. I believe I was chosen because I was enthusiastic and showed the initiative to take on something new. I believe that I had also proved I could work an unconventional schedule and accomplish the work. At the time, virtual reference was innovative and unclaimed territory. I found it interesting and delved into learning all aspects of it. Eventually more libraries across the state began adding virtual reference. The state library took notice and implemented a statewide virtual reference service—NCknows. Once they had a new way to serve their patrons, they needed someone to manage the service. I didn't consciously seek the position, but I had shown my enthusiasm and gotten myself noticed. I had also created a good track record of doing what I said I was going to do.

Someone at a higher level had noticed my work, because I was offered the position to manage the new service. I believe this happened because I had made myself stand out in the field. One of the ways I did so was by cutting through the library jargon and translating the information into a more user-friendly language for new users. I think those who try to cling to library jargon are perpetuating a form of penguinism, or "This is the way we do things." In today's world, library staff must stretch themselves in new ways. It is no longer acceptable to believe patrons should learn our ways.

The virtual reference position was unique in that I was now a private contractor. While the position was considered part-time, the salary was competitive with my full-time salary at the academic library. I was able to work in librarianship and still have time for the arts work I loved. While this was attractive to me, few librarians find themselves in this spot and even fewer want to be. The advantage to jobs like mine is that they offer unconventional lifestyle options and usually pay a higher salary due to lack of benefits. For me, it meant leaving the library office, a basement bunker of cubicles, bad light, and strange humming noises. I was more than ready to do that. This gave me the autonomy I craved and the chance to be on the cutting edge that I had been missing. For the next eight years I worked from home, a freedom that fit my personal and professional needs.

NONPENGUIN REALITIES

To the roughly 30 percent of librarians who are unionized, job security can be significant and deeply important. In the past few years, we've seen the downside of nonunionized employment in libraries. Layoffs swept through some public libraries in my state in chaotic fashion, leaving families and long-term employees in a state of confusion. A private contractor's job is usually renewed annually. While this creates some insecurity, it has allowed me to diversify my skills and pursue multiple careers. This can provide a cushion in case one job is eliminated.

While this was the perfect job for me, it would not be the perfect one for others. Before pursuing a position outside of a library, it's important to know yourself and your work habits. Working outside of an office, away from people, can be very disorienting. Over the years I've had to discover my own discipline and work ethic as well as some tricks to keep myself on task. I have also had to learn how to live in a home that is also an office. While these may seem like small things, they can be major obstacles if you are easily distractible. It's important to remember that you still have a job and that you owe an employer a certain amount of completed work, regardless of your work location.

Surprisingly, the danger of working from home can be that one works too much and not too little. Without clear starting and stopping times, work can melt into an all-day affair and eat into weekends. In my case, I discovered that I work best in the morning and the late afternoon and evening, so I force myself to take time off in the afternoon. In talking with other freelancers, I know the problem of setting boundaries with time can blossom into a full-blown crisis if not dealt with effectively. A friend in a similar position has a clock that he uses to "clock in" and "clock out" so he can better focus when at "work." Reverse penguinism? Perhaps, but sometimes unconventional jobs require you to revert back to conventional or penguinish ways.

While anyone working as a contractor will have to be his or her own tech support, I have found this works to my advantage. It forces me to remain savvy with technology, which is a desirable trait should I return to a library workplace. Employers often support the effort to stay proficient in technology by enabling you to bill for this in your contract. Technology classes are offered both in person and online. It's important to keep a list of the skills that you need to do your job and make sure you maintain those skills. Take advantage of professional development opportunities offered by your employer's library or by professional organizations in your area.

One of the best tools I use is a collaborative virtual reference electronic mailing list whose members are people with jobs like mine. Unconventional positions mean that there aren't many others who share similar experiences, so cultivate the ones who do, and be open and informal in your communications with them. Whenever something happens that makes me doubt my sanity, I go to them. In addition, I have an advisory board made up of colleagues throughout the state that I rely on for honest advice. Finally, I have one or two librarians I lean on often, whether it is to get their reaction to wild ideas or discuss long-term career questions. Remember, just because you are not a penguin doesn't mean that you won't occasionally need to find "some of your own kind." No one will understand you as clearly as someone in your situation.

Removing yourself from a library doesn't mean that you should remove yourself from the library family. One way to remain connected is by attending conferences. I always find my time at conferences and remote trainings useful. Getting to see a colleague is different from exchanging e-mails. In recent years, I've also found speaking on the phone can be more effective than e-mailing. Many introverts find working at home or by themselves attractive, but it may mean a stronger need to deal with others than at the traditional workplace. In my case, I've found I've had to reach out more to people and in more personal ways than before.

ADVANTAGES OF NONPENGUINISM

I'm able to coordinate my own schedule to take advantage of simple things—like a sunny day. I've discovered my own work rhythms and am able to accommodate them, instead of having to plow through a nine-to-five schedule. I've worked on NCknows while on vacation and can travel freely as long as project timelines are met and shifts covered. I've helped patrons from the coast while in the mountains, and patrons from the mountains while looking out at the beach.

One asset to being an independent contractor that has been a pleasant surprise to me is my ability to advance the profession. In my case, the state of North Carolina was able to offer an experimental flexible program that has helped thousands of patrons. My role has shifted over the years to accommodate the program. I have a strong sense of ownership of this program. For someone who doesn't want to be a penguin, the opportunity to be out in front can be very rewarding. While you won't

get to make all of the key decisions, you will have a much better chance of being part of new
creations.

The other important thing
for me is that my work isn't
one in a series of professional
projects. It is my business, and
I appreciate the opportunity to
rise to the challenges that this
presents. In addition, I am able
to consult and pursue other projects as my time permits. This has
encouraged an entrepreneur-
ial spirit and has given me the

How to Avoid Penguinism

- Plan for an unconventional work situation.
- Be proactive and make things happen.
- Bring change and create independence.
- Identify something that excites you and pursue it as employment.
- Maintain contact with colleagues about potential unconventional jobs.
- Seek innovative and unclaimed territory.

---

freedom and confidence to consider other initiatives I would not have been able to
pursue otherwise. This is not to say that all libraries are restrictive. However, most
positions come with a fixed set of responsibilities and, after those are completed,
often little time for other initiatives. Plus, I no longer have to stare at the clock just
to satisfy an overly bureaucratic idea of a work schedule. My time is my own, to use
as effectively and efficiently as I can.

CONSIDER THE POSSIBILITIES

New changes in technology have created new possibilities in work conditions in
many professions. Libraries have long been friendly work environments for a whole
host of alternative and unconventional people. The truth of the matter is that there
is a lot of penguinism in most jobs. The trick is for each employee to find what works
for him or her. Librarians can help themselves by clearly articulating which aspects
of their work conditions they find liberating—flex time, working from home, and so
on. They also have greater opportunities to choose the types of jobs that work best
for them. The key for me in finding my path was to recognize the type of job that was
best for me and to have the courage to pursue that path.

WHAT IF THE JOB DOESN'T WORK OUT?

Kelly Evans

Accepting a new position can be both exciting and scary. The first days are full of meeting new people and becoming acclimated to a new environment. As things settle down and the excitement fades, reality sets in. The reality may be that the new job is not right for you. What do you do if you find yourself in this situation? How do you proceed if you discover that you want out? How do you deal with finding a new job when there are bound to be questions about why you are leaving your current position? This chapter examines how to assess a situation when you are faltering, how to turn negatives into positives, and how to move on to the next phase of your career.

A BOX OF CHOCOLATES

> My momma always said, "Life was like a box of chocolates.
> You never know what you're gonna get."
>
> —*Forrest Gump*

Comparatively, interviewing and taking a new job is also like the chocolates sampler. You don't know exactly what that new job will be and how you will fit into the organization until you arrive.

My journey began when I interviewed for a position in a subject-specific library that would involve working with a small team of librarians. The position was in an ARL (Association of Research Libraries) library, it was tenure-track, and it offered a good salary and benefits. In addition, it was located in a great college town. On paper, the job was everything that I wanted. When I interviewed in person, it seemed a perfect fit too.

The position was as liaison to a department that previously did not have a relationship with this particular campus library. For the interview, I was asked to devise a plan of how I could serve as liaison to this academic department. I viewed this as a once-in-a-lifetime opportunity to create a new liaison program from scratch and to incorporate inventive instructional opportunities. I devoted considerable research to devising initiatives for a three-year plan that I thought was well crafted to meet the needs of the department.

The interview went well, and I was offered the position. I was delighted and accepted enthusiastically. It seemed I would have autonomy, support, and a chance to be innovative and to try out new ideas. As soon as I arrived, I began to implement the plan that I had outlined in my interview. In hindsight, I see that I interpreted being hired as a green light to pursue initiatives I had presented during the interview. Instead of proceeding gradually and checking with my supervisor, I began putting my proposal into action. I introduced myself to my new colleagues in my department and began to make plans for working with them. At first, I was unaware that some of my initiatives were not well received by everyone. It seemed that some library colleagues were pleased with my independence and happy that I was collaborating with faculty and creating new programming; others were less enthused. In fact, some of my initiatives were seen as creating additional work for the library and putting a strain on resources.

I first became aware of problems when I was asked to inform and copy others on e-mails I sent to faculty in my academic department. I was also asked to refrain from communicating with department heads and professors without consulting specific people in the library. This deflated some of my enthusiasm, but it did not register with me that I might have seriously overstepped some boundaries. This was probably the moment I should have reassessed my plans to make sure they fit with the organization's plans, but I was so involved in working with my department that I didn't step back and reassess. Over time, I felt tensions building and began to feel uncertain about discussing new ideas with coworkers. This left me feeling isolated and unclear about what I should or should not be doing.

At the same time that I was adjusting to new work requirements, I was under pressure to publish as part of my goal to obtain tenure. By the end of the first year, I was failing to meet this mandate. I realize now that I didn't know how to proceed and that I needed mentoring. At the time, however, I was simply struggling and failing to meet the expectation. This created additional stress for me as well as in my working relationships with others.

As tensions escalated, I realized I had to take action. I began by meeting with individuals in library management in an attempt to resolve problems and to return myself to a better footing. Unfortunately, even after several meetings, some issues remained unresolved. By the time any work situation reaches this point, there is bound to be frustration and resentment all around. I was disappointed because I did not feel I was always being heard. I am certain that others in the library were equally frustrated with me. In situations like this, both parties may be more intent on having their say and being heard than in listening carefully to what the other is saying. This can lead to further frustration and make a bad work situation worse.

Because we didn't seem to be making progress, I decided to pursue some self-education to try to turn the situation around. I began by looking at the guidelines for my job, as well as university and faculty policies governing personnel relations. I also took advantage of university workshops about conflict in the workplace and other personnel issues. The workshops included ways to communicate more effectively and addressed appropriate supervisor–employee relationships. They also pointed out different work styles. This information was very helpful because it showed me that I had a lot to learn about work styles and different work situations. Obviously, I could not go up to an individual and announce that I attended this workshop and had learned "This is why you are the way you are." The purpose of the workshop was to help *me* handle the situation with more awareness. The workshops allowed me to gain perspective on how my actions might be interfering with situations or even making matters worse.

The workshops also made me aware of other options. One thing all employees should know is that, if the situation cannot be easily resolved at your level, you have the right to take the matter to university human resources or to a personnel manager in the library. Bringing in human resources can be beneficial for mediating a situation when there is a communication breakdown. Before you reach this point, however, it is wise to meet with the human resources representative individually to discuss what has happened and the steps you have taken and are currently taking. Try to be as calm as possible. Yes, you may shed a few tears, but be composed to the extent possible. Emotions have a way of clouding perspectives and making it difficult to hear the advice you are given.

In fact, dealing with emotions can become a major hurdle anytime there is workplace stress. This is when it is important to remember that although a challenging workplace situation can seem like the end of the world, it is not. Try to maintain perspective and to remind yourself that everyone involved wants to do a good job; people simply have different approaches. Also, remember to take care of yourself emotionally and physically. Look for ways to relieve stress through outside activities that help you refocus your energy to the positive. Also, talking to family, friends, former mentors, or others outside the work environment can help soften what you are experiencing. We are all guilty of venting at work, but it is not productive, and what you say can travel back to the person about whom you are complaining.

In hindsight, I see that I did not always keep things in balance. The problems at work made me start to doubt myself. I worried that I had ruined my career and that I would never recover. I also doubted that the steps I was taking to "fix" the problems were working. I did not see a path to resolution, and I suspected that all parties were entrenched in their positions. There didn't seem to be any avenues left open that would put me back where I needed to be. It was then that I realized I did not have a future in that library, that I needed to start fresh in a place that was a better fit for me. That is when I started planning to leave my position.

The realization that I had to leave the job created additional stress. There is no way around the fact that it is discouraging when things don't turn out the way you hoped. However, I tried to look at the experience as a lesson learned. While this wasn't always easy in the beginning, I was determined to build on these lessons going forward.

I was reassured by the fact that my subject specialty experience would help me in applying for jobs because my experience and qualifications were in demand. I also felt confident in my interviewing skills, so I was not nervous about job hunting. Still, I did have to readjust my thinking to let go of where I was and to look toward a different future than the one I had envisioned.

Even though I was getting ready to look for another job, I still had a job to do, and I still had something to contribute to the organization. I was determined to perform my duties well until the last day. I continued to teach, help students and faculty, and be committed to what I love doing—librarianship. I also viewed this time as an opportunity to improve my skills and résumé, so I took on new projects. Specifically, I undertook the responsibility of supervising graduate students, and I worked with departmental faculty on collaborative research projects. This was not only a way to improve my skills; working on these projects kept me from dwelling on disappointment.

Regardless of where my new job might be, I knew it was to my benefit to maintain research partnerships with faculty and colleagues. To accomplish this, I worked with a colleague in an academic department on a feasibility analysis course. The project involved my role as an embedded librarian and researching how innovative technological space and collaboration can enhance learning. This research led to a publication and might be an opportunity I would have missed if I had simply "checked out" once I realized that I would be leaving. It also gave me something positive and rewarding on which to focus my energies.

In addition, I took advantage of training opportunities in the workplace that could carry over to my next job. For instance, I learned about data curation, knowledge that I may have use for in a future job. Taking workshops and cementing relationships certainly helped me, but I also believe it made things go smoother with my coworkers because they realized I was still engaged. And don't think that your coworkers don't know what is happening. Even if they don't officially know, the rumor mill will keep them up to date. Don't contribute to that rumor mill by confiding details to your colleagues. Keep your relationships professional. If you need to talk to someone, talk to former colleagues and mentors and ask that they maintain confidence.

BEFORE AN INTERVIEW

Acknowledging that I was not going to remain in my position meant that I had to start the job search over again. Before I undertook this, I sat down and mapped out a strategy that has served me well and could work well for others. First, I contacted my references to let them know that I might need them as references in the near future. Next, I pulled out my résumé and looked for ways to strengthen it. I made sure that all of my current work duties and experiences were up to date. The next step was to make good use of conferences as places to network. Even if you attend a conference to learn about new trends in librarianship, it can also be the ideal time to network with potential employers. I especially recommend targeting social networking opportunities like open houses and after-hours committee gatherings. These are informal, low-pressure places to make face-to-face contact. Finally, I wrote out a list of what I wanted from a future employer. I focused on aspects that I could clearly articulate, rather than vague concepts like "I want a good job."

> ### Tips for the Job Search
>
> - Contact references.
> - Strengthen your résumé.
> - Network at conferences.
> - List expectations for future employers.
> - Prepare positive responses to probing interview questions.

As I embarked on a new job search, I reviewed what questions to expect in interviews. I looked at questions I would be asked as well as the questions I wanted answered. I created questions that would help me get to the heart of what I, as an employee, was seeking in a position and an organization.

Before you ever begin a job search you should ask yourself some questions: What type of position are you seeking? Do you want a tenure-track position with its associated responsibilities? How much supervision are you comfortable with? Do you prefer communicating via e-mail or face-to-face? Do you want a mentor assigned to you, or would you prefer to choose one? Knowing what your requirements are can help you eliminate positions that aren't right for you. You don't want to end up in a job that isn't the right fit.

WHAT TO LOOK FOR IN AN INTERVIEW

The academic interviewing process can be hectic and overwhelming. You may be scheduled to meet with twenty or so people, including various groups and committees. You will probably meet with the dean or director of the library and sometimes the dean of a college. Your time with your potential direct supervisor may be limited to a brief meeting or lunch. Use whatever time you have to observe how well you and that person interact together. While it can be difficult to reach a deep understanding with limited contact, you can get a sense of how you and the other person relate. Also, look at how well departments function together and separately. This can give further insight into how the organization is run.

Some questions to ask the supervisor in order to solicit interpersonal dynamics in the organization include these:

- What is your management style?
- How do you address conflict and issues in your department?
- What level of autonomy does an employee have, and when should he or she step back and allow the supervisor to take control of a situation?
- What is your preferred method of day-to-day communication?
- Is the setting team oriented or more individualized work?
- How often should the employee meet with the supervisor?

Once you have asked a question, listen carefully to what is said and not said. Also observe body language. If a potential supervisor seems uncomfortable with certain questions, this could tell you something important. Along with observing body language, try to get past the general to the specific. When possible, ask for examples, as these are a good way of judging a situation for yourself instead of simply being told, "There was a conflict but I resolved it." Be attentive to the environment and see if what you observe matches with what you are being told. For instance, many places claim to be team oriented, but you should observe how others interact and how they treat you. Do they treat you as a future member of their team, or do they seem aloof or cliquish?

In addition to observing potential colleagues, show an interest in them. Ask about their publications and other scholarly works. In fact, it's a good idea to look them up beforehand to see what they have published and where they have presented. Not only does this give you a sense of what the institution values, but it can provide an opening to start a conversation with a potential colleague.

Find out what organizations or associations matter to your supervisor and/or to the library administration. Do they care about statewide library organizations, or do they value only national and international associations? How much support can the library give you to participate, whether through travel funds or with release time to serve on committees within these organizations.

If the position you are interviewing for is a tenure-track position and you are new to tenure, meaning you have no clue how the whole process works, tenure can be an obstacle course. Most tenure-granting institutions allow five to six years to achieve tenure. In some cases, the library's tenure policies are separate from the university's tenure process. In other cases, particularly in ARL libraries, the tenure process is on par with other departmental faculty. Because not all tenure is the same, it is important that you ask pertinent questions to help you decide if the library's tenure process is right for you.

You also want to understand the annual review and tenure review process. Your supervisor will review you annually, but sometimes other library faculty are part of the process. Tenure review is usually ongoing in the first three years. After that, there may be one review before you actually go up for tenure. Finding out how you are reviewed and who reviews you is essential to success in your career. If this is not clearly articulated, you may feel frustrated and uncertain about what you are expected to accomplish.

Always get an idea of the quantity of peer-reviewed publications expected. Even if the answer is "We don't have a number," the reality is that they usually have a number in mind. You could end up taking a job and discover later that there is an absolute requirement for one peer-reviewed article per year.

Ask about mentoring. Your chances of achieving tenure could be greater if you have someone to mentor you who has experience in the tenure process and who cares about seeing you succeed. Tenure track requires an advocate who knows your work and can help you navigate the process. Once you have been in a job for a while, you may be allowed to choose your own mentor.

WHY DID YOU LEAVE?

Ah, the question on every interviewer's mind. "Why did you leave your current job?" No matter what the situation, never make negative statements about the workplace you are leaving. You don't have to give details of your work experience or name people. In fact, you should not. However, trying to avoid the question also doesn't work. This is the moment for some simple honesty. "Unfortunately, it wasn't the right fit." If pressed to explain why, I would give the simple answer: "I found the tenure process challenging, and I wanted a position that would let me focus all my energies on providing the best service possible to the students." This opens the door to divert the conversation back to the current position because you can expand to say, "That is what interested me about this position." Interviewers are watching you to see how you respond to difficult questions. Answering with dignity and without pointing an accusatory finger at anyone always gets points.

In today's environment, no one will fault you if you want to leave your current position. In the past, people often stayed in positions for many years, but this is no longer true. Potential employers want to know that you can overcome a negative experience and that you are excited about coming to work for their organization. They also want to be reassured that you are not bringing baggage with you.

WHEN THE TIME COMES TO LEAVE

Once I accepted a new job and knew when I was leaving, I wanted to let the departmental faculty know that I was leaving and where I was going. I stressed that I would like to continue to work together on articles and other projects. I was fortunate to have strong working relationships with faculty that could continue. No matter what work situation you find yourself in, do not burn bridges. There are positives in any work environment and good people to be your support system. Even as my time was winding down, I made it a point to attend faculty meetings and to engage in conversation with everyone. I wanted to stay positive and engaged with my colleagues until the end.

STARTING A NEW JOB WITH BAGGAGE

I did find a new job and was ready to make a fresh start. However, I still felt a variety of emotions about my previous job. How to handle this? Starting any new position is stressful. A new employee must learn workplace dynamics, politics, and the university system. You may be asked this question: "How did they do things where you were before?" It is fine to admit it was not the right fit, but always remain professional in talking about your experiences. Take the positives from your previous experiences and apply them to your new environment. Be open to the way things are done in your current situation. Your new job may be at an institution or library with less funding and resources than your previous library. It was an adjustment for me to move from a specialized library environment into a main library, but going in with a positive attitude helped make the transition smoother.

No matter what happens or how things turn out with a job experience, have no regrets. Taking any job is a risk, but out of every risky situation comes a new learning experience and an opportunity you would have missed if you had looked too hard before you leaped.

HAPPILY EVER AFTER, RIGHT? WELL . . .

So the story ends happily ever after, right? New job. New place. Everything is perfect.

Not so fast. As I was writing this chapter, I was informed that my new position was being eliminated because of state budget cuts. Therefore, I will have to move on again. After the stress of the past two years and the loss of my new position, you might think I would have trouble coping with this latest setback. Actually, my past experience prepared me to better handle this job loss. I already have strategies for job seeking in place. Two days after I was given the news, I began applying for positions. I contacted former colleagues and references and explained the situation. Within a week I had five e-mails from several people sending me the same job posting. Having the support system to move on and find another job is critical to the success of my career.

So my career path has been filled with unforeseen trials. I have tasted every chocolate in Forrest Gump's box of chocolates. I cannot say that I have enjoyed every moment of the experience, but I can say that there is value in every experience. I have gained wisdom and a broader understanding of how organizations work. I have had the opportunity to look closely at my personal goals and to tailor my job searches toward what is meaningful to me.

AFTERWORD

It is impossible to cover in detail all aspects of a library career because career paths can be vastly different. Our goal in this book was to address some common issues and offer advice from experienced professionals in the field. We recruited authors from a variety of libraries to bring a wide range of skills and experiences. While not every chapter may speak to your situation, we hope you found nuggets of wisdom to help you in the future.

What is the future? The Bureau of Labor Statistics' *Occupational Outlook Handbook* predicts that employment of librarians will grow 7 percent from 2010 to 2020 (www .bls.gov/ooh/education-training-and-library/librarians.htm). They acknowledge that job hunters could face strong competition early in the decade but that prospects will improve later in the decade as older librarians retire. This means that there will be new career opportunities, both at the entry level and beyond, with the prospect to move up the librarianship ladder. We hope this book has provided strategies and skills to help you take advantage of this growth in the field of librarianship.

Even if you choose not to work in a library or are not able to find a job in a library, it is good to know that your skills have wide application, as detailed in chapter 8. The *Occupational Outlook Handbook* states that librarians' "research and analytical skills are valuable for jobs in a variety of other fields, such as market researchers or computer and information systems managers" (www.bls.gov/ooh/education-training-and-library/librarians.htm#tab-6).

Finally, we sincerely hope that you enjoyed reading this book as much as we enjoyed compiling and editing it. We worked with many great authors and were amazed at what they knew and had to offer. We learned a great deal and hope that you have too.

Lois Stickell and Bridgette Sanders

CONTRIBUTORS

TAMARA ACEVEDO is library and legal research manager for the law firm of Moore & Van Allen, PLLC. In this position she manages all aspects of the law firm's legal research needs including collection development and supervising the library department. Prior to joining Moore & Van Allen, Tamara held various positions at Atkins Library at the University of North Carolina at Charlotte. Tamara received a bachelor of arts degree in criminal justice from the University of North Carolina at Charlotte in 1998. She was awarded a master of library science from the University of South Carolina in 2007. A native of Advance, North Carolina, Tamara is the wife of Angel and proud mother of one daughter, Desirae.

PHIL BLANK has worked for the last eight years as the statewide coordinator of the NCknows project for the State Library of North Carolina. He has worked in public, community college, and large academic libraries since graduating from the MLS program at UNC Chapel Hill. He recently finished reading *The Journals of Spalding Gray*.

JENNY DALE is first year instruction coordinator at the University of North Carolina at Greensboro's University Libraries. In addition to coordinating and teaching library instruction for 100-level classes, she is the liaison to the English Department, the Kinesiology Department, and the First Year Experience program. In addition to her teaching and liaison work, Jenny is also actively involved in campus outreach. She received her MSLS from the University of North Carolina at Chapel Hill. In her free time, Jenny likes to read literary fiction, young adult novels, and the occasional mystery.

KELLY EVANS is a business librarian and assistant professor at Eastern Washington University in Spokane, Washington. She received her MLS from Indiana University in 2004 and her BA in history from Virginia Wesleyan College in 2001. Kelly likes to read political and social commentaries, and her favorite author is Bill Bryson.

KATHERINE FARMER is director of the Curriculum Materials Center and education research and instruction librarian at Murray State University in Kentucky. When she is not busy managing the Curriculum Materials Center and assisting students and faculty with their research needs, Katherine is also the coordinator of the Racer Children's Materials Preview Center at Waterfield Library. She holds an MLIS from the University of Southern Mississippi and began her library career as an elementary school librarian. She enjoys reading children's literature and mysteries.

Lynda Kellam is the data services and government information librarian at the University of North Carolina at Greensboro's University Libraries. In addition to providing research assistance and instruction on data and government sources, she is the library instruction and collections liaison to the Political Science Department, Environmental Studies program, and Pre-Law program. In her spare time she is a co-coordinator of the Reference Department's LIS graduate student intern program and teaches a world politics class for the Political Science Department. She received her MA in political science from the University of Wisconsin–Madison, and her MLIS from the University of North Carolina at Greensboro. She reads mostly history and nonfiction, but her favorite author is Haruki Murakami.

MELINDA LIVAS is distance services librarian for C. G. O'Kelly Library, Winston Salem State University. She provides virtual library services and resources to distance learners and faculty members. Her research interests include infusing pedagogy and andragogy with technology. Her favorite authors are John Grisham and Thomas Friedman. She also follows Meredith Farkas's blog, *Information Wants to Be Free.*

BETH MARTIN is Charlotte program coordinator for the UNC Greensboro Library and Information Studies Program. She coordinates the distance education program for UNC Greensboro and teaches the Foundation, Information Literacy, and Academic Library courses in the program. Beth obtained her MLIS from UNC Greensboro and is currently pursuing a PhD in adult education at North Carolina State University. She loves science fiction, fantasy, and mystery while her favorite authors include Neil Gaiman, Octavia Butler, and P. D. James.

ANNIE PAYTON is director of library services at Alabama A&M University. Annie's library interest includes archives and information literacy. She received her MLS and PhD from the University of Southern Mississippi. Documenting and preserving the history of the past and future piques her interest in libraries and archival studies. In addition to managing the daily operations of Hunt Library, Annie is an adjunct professor in the College of Education. Her teaching interests include Reading in the Content Area, Educational Assessment and Children's Literature. Annie has more than twenty-five years of experience in library services. She considers herself an astute innovative builder in the efficient management of library programs.

THEODOSIA SHIELDS is director of library services at North Carolina Central University. She received her MLS degree from Atlanta University and her PhD from the University of Pittsburgh. She has more than twenty-five years of experience in library administration and management in various public and private academic institutions. The delivery of quality information service and transforming libraries to better serve users has been her ultimate goal in each leadership role. She is affiliated with many professional organizations on a local, regional, and national level.

GRETA WOOD is assistant professor/business reference librarian and library liaison to the Shackouls Honors College at Mississippi State University Libraries. She received her master's degree in library and information studies from The University of North Carolina at Greensboro, her master's degree in English from The University of North Carolina at Charlotte, her bachelor's degree in English from Colby College in Waterville, Maine, and is currently pursuing an MBA through Mississippi State University's Distance MBA Program. Authors she enjoys reading include Jim Butcher, Tana French, Jo Nesbo, Carol O'Connell and Minette Waters.

INDEX